PART 1   MEDIAEVAL AND RENAISSANCE ART
by Catherine King

CONTENTS

1   Mediaeval European art   7
    (i)   Northern-European, Roman and Byzantine variations of the
          style of Late Imperial Rome: the art of isolation   7
    (ii) Pan-European styles: Carolingian, Ottonian, Romanesque and
          Gothic   11

2   Mediaeval Italian and, in particular, Tuscan art   13

3   Comparison and contrast between mediaeval and Renaissance art
    and its organization: an introduction to the debate of Units 8–13
    based on Section I of Elizabeth G. Holt (ed.) (1957) *A Documentary
    History of Art*, Volume I, Doubleday (set book)   20

    Figures 1–51   29

Arts: A Second Level Course

Renaissance and Reformation
Course Supplement

Mediaeval European Background

Prepared for the Course Team by Catherine King, Margaret and Peter Spufford, Noel Coley and Brian Stone

Supervisory Reader: Francis Clark

The Open University Press

Cover illustration:

The Open University Press
Walton Hall, Milton Keynes, MK7 6AA

First published 1975
Copyright © 1975 The Open University

Designed by the Media Development Group of The Open University.

Printed in Great Britain by
EYRE AND SPOTTISWOODE LIMITED
AT GROSVENOR PRESS, PORTSMOUTH

ISBN 0 335 00675 2

This text forms part of an Open University course. The complete list of units in the course appears at the end of this text.

For general availability of supporting material referred to in this text, please write to the Director of Marketing, The Open University, P.O. Box 81, Walton Hall, Milton Keynes, MK7 6AT.

Further information on Open University courses may be obtained from the Admissions Office, The Open University, P.O. Box 48, Walton Hall, Milton Keynes, MK7 6AB.

1.1

GENERAL INTRODUCTION

This new double unit is designed both to supplement and to shorten this course, which has proved, over the four years of its operation, to be a heavy one for students. Units 3–4, 14 and 28 have been withdrawn and study of them will be replaced in the following way:

1 Part 2 of this course supplement replaces units 3–4. The set books and general background reading list stay the same.

2 You will receive in due course a reading guide to Machiavelli's *The Prince*, which remains a set book. The general background reading list to this remains valid.

3 *An Introduction to Elizabethan England* (Unit 28) is not being replaced for 1976.

Our general aim is to provide you at the outset with a fuller idea of mediaeval Europe as a background to Renaissance Studies, so that you may better understand the Renaissance itself. There is no specific work here on the Reformation, the origins of which are fully covered in Units 20–21. The five contributors have made some effort to integrate their work, although this may not always be indicated by cross-references.

Part 1, by Catherine King, supplements the mediaeval background material in existing art history units, but also does much more. Catherine King's first section is an historical essay on the development of Europe from the end of the Roman Empire to the beginning of our period, viewed through what one might call a perspective of art and architecture. Seen in this way, such matters as the artistic and social development of Christianity, the invasions of Europe from north and south, the different qualities of southern and north-western Europe, and the interaction of paganism and Christianity, supplement existing material on the classical heritage. The second section gives an idea of the diversity of mediaeval Italian art, and concentrates on Tuscany, and the third, by way of introduction to the debate of Units 8–13, draws comparisons and contrasts between mediaeval and Renaissance Italian art.

Part 2, by Margaret and Peter Spufford, contains new material on European society, economy and population patterns during the period 1300–1600, and should be used in conjunction with the set books, Hay, and Koenigsberger and Mosse.

Part 3, by Noel Coley, is entitled 'The Late Mediaeval World Picture'. It formally supplements Units 5–6 and provides an introduction and some background to Units 15–16, as well as bringing together, in an introductory manner, material which appears later in the course and is dealt with in greater detail. It should give you a preliminary idea of how to look at the universe through mediaeval eyes, and thus prepare you to grapple with the changes in scientific knowledge which came with the Renaissance. A measure of interdisciplinary treatment brings matters religious, literary and artistic within the compass of the argument.

Part 4, by Brian Stone, supplements the background to the study of Elizabethan poetry and drama in Units 5–6, 29–34, and corrects the balance of Unit 6, in which there is too much emphasis on allegory, to the neglect of other important matters. It contains an essay on attitudes towards, and activities in, the performing arts, in the Europe of our period, and gives some background to mediaeval lyric poetry and its main body of inspirational ideas, those connected with courtly love.

Now, how do you use this new material, and when do you read it? I suggest the following study programme:

1   After reading Units 1–2, read Part 1 straight through, concentrating on gaining a first illumination concerning a wide sweep of history, and a first acquaintance with styles of art and architecture which will help you when you come to history of art units for detailed work.

2   Read Part 2 carefully and in your two set books, Hay: *Europe in the Four-teenth and Fifteenth Centuries*[1], and Koenigsberger and Mosse: *Europe in the Sixteenth Century*[2], take note of the following at appropriate times in this study:

Hay pp. 26–31 (conditions in the countryside of Europe)
        71–4 (the urban classes)
        45–60 (the church)
        31–5 (population, plague and the economy)
        359–94 (trade)
Koenigsberger and Mosse pp. 54–9 (conditions in the towns)
                                  21–53 (prices and wages).

3   Read Part 3, doing your best to absorb the material there which is new to you, but don't allow difficulties to hold you up.

4   Read existing Units 5–6 straight through; I now indicate with what emphasis and concentration you might read the separate parts, and also how they relate to the new material:

Sections 1–2 *Introduction and The Middle Ages:* read quickly.
        3 *The Revival of Classical Learning in Italy:* read quickly. Pay close attention to Petrarch.
        4 *Education:* study with care.
    5.1–5.5 *Renaissance Neo-Platonism:* read in conjunction with Noel
    and 6.1 Coley's new work (paras. 332–356).
        7 *Mediaeval Allegory.* Read quickly. But if you don't do all the exercises, make sure that you can define and recognize literary allegory.
        8 *Renaissance Allegory:* this subject is treated more fully later. Read quickly, but don't miss the television programme (no. 3).
        9 *The Middle Ages and the Renaissance:* read with care.
  Appendix *Everyman:* probably it will be best to leave this until you study it in connection with the Reformation and television programme 11, which is wholly concerned with it.

5   Read Part 4 of the new material with care. You will find that the first section, on the performing arts, lends itself to continuous reading, but please spend as much time as you can afford on the poetry, which concludes the supplementary double unit.

[1] Hay, D., *Europe in the Fourteenth and Fifteenth Centuries*, Longman, 1966, (set book).
[2] Koenigsberger, H. G., and Mosse, G. L., *Europe in the Sixteenth Century*, Longman, 1968 (set book).

1 MEDIAEVAL EUROPEAN ART

(i) Northern-European, Roman and Byzantine variations of the style of Late Imperial Rome: the art of isolation

101 What happened to European art during the thousand years after the fall of the western Roman Empire? Generalizing only too daringly, I can say that the styles, forms, function and techniques of Roman art, which had as many transmutations of classical and hellenistic Greek modes as there were provinces in the Empire, were revolutionized, adapted and sometimes even forgotten. New centres of artistic production emerged, at first in those areas isolated from the chaos of the rest of Europe. Then, as 'barbarians' settled into the landscape and became 'natives', they created new cultural centres in northern Europe (the heartland of the great mediaeval styles of Romanesque and Gothic). These centres borrowed from and were intimately linked with the old Mediterranean artistic centres (which were themselves products of a new ethos – Christian Byzantium and Rome, not pagan Greece, Asia-Minor and Latium) through their shared Christian culture, but were truly independent creations or perhaps 'mutations' nevertheless. Despite its enthusiasm for the classical past and its frequently genuine belief that it was recreating the styles of antiquity, Christian Italy in the fifteenth century was the product of a 'new world'.

How did the artistic transformation occur? As I proceed in my generalizations I want to give some examples illustrating the changes that took place. Keep in mind that, like the generalizations, these are a useful but rather selective guide to your thinking about mediaeval art – not the 'last word'.

Historians of Roman art usually see the process of declassicizing Imperial art as beginning in at least the early second century, ascribing it to the cultural feedback from the various subjugated, but always tolerated cultures of the Empire, to the dislocation of society in the later Empire (only *just* containing invasion of its borders and split by fights over Imperial succession), and perhaps also to the growth of mystery religions, among them Christianity and Mithraism with their emotionalism and spirituality. This process (I give an exercise comparing the symbolic and 'expressionistic' tendencies of 'mediaeval' art with the naturalistic, though still idealized concepts of classical art in Unit 10, pp. 88–93) was accelerated by three events. Two of them were decisions made by Constantine in the early fourth century – to make Christianity the official religion of the Empire (whilst tolerating others) and to move his capital from Rome to Constantinople, leaving the western Empire largely unprotected against the third event: the invasion of northern barbarian tribes between the fourth and the eighth centuries, and of the Arab armies at the end of that period. The latter decision, was in fact a 'correct' one: Constantinople didn't fall for a thousand years.

102 The remaining mosaics in the vault of the early fourth-century mausoleum of Costanza in Rome (Figure 1) show how strongly Early Christian art was linked to that of pagan Rome. The technique is one practised in previous centuries. The white background with its ebullient decoration of flora and fauna – in a Persian carpet pattern – had been well-established by the middle of the second century in imperial Rome. In details – the cupids treading grapes and bringing in the harvest – the iconography has been adapted from Dionysiac traditions. We might, of course, feel a little differently about the decoration if the dome mosaic – representing the Four Rivers of Paradise – had survived.

The character, customs and habits which distinguish a people or community from others;

103   The church of Santa Sabina in Rome is a good example of the Christian architecture of the Late Empire whose forms were to be so influential (Figures 2–3). It has a bare façade balanced by an originally very rich interior (the very opposite principle is employed in Roman and Greek temples). Looking at the illustrations, try to describe the structure.

It is a simple rectangular hall with an apse on one of its shorter ends, and a door on the short end opposite it. In the apse the bishop would preside. In front was (and is) the altar. It might have had five but here there are three aisles, with one of them (the nave) larger and with a higher roof allowing light to enter. The nave roof is flat and wooden, the side aisle roofs slope. They were simply tiled outside. The *basilican* form, of which this is a typical example, was a suitable form for Christian architects to use because it had been the form used by Roman architects (but *not* Greeks) for administrative legal structures. Then, the apse and opposing doorway were sometimes on the long sides, and the tribunal of the Judge or even Emperor was its focus beneath the apse. The tribunal was replaced by the Christian altar – in all extant basilicas, under an apse on one of the short sides of the hall shape. It seems that the basilican form was taken over by Christian architects because it was suitable for the assembly of very large congregations: for the earliest basilicas were few in number and the original first four Constantinian basilicas of Rome were intended to be able to hold *all* the Christians in Rome at one time. The growing secular power of the Church and its increasingly rigid hierarchy helps to explain the very commanding representations of holy figures in Early mediaeval art – much more awesome than the little Christ sculpted on the unique fifth-century wooden doors of Santa Sabina (Figures 4–5), who is represented in the pose used by earlier Imperial artists for an orator or magistrate making a speech. It helps too to explain that rigid sense of place and importance you will notice in some of the other scenes on these doors, where angelic figures are huge, and where the scenes are neatly stratified – for instance Christ is separated by palm trees (these aren't in the gospel accounts) from the two prophets of the *Transfiguration*. The institutionalization of the church and the powerful social and temporal role thrust on to it by events also helps explain the modifications of the basilican form. Transepts might be added to emphasize the importance of the altar and apse, and to seat singers or clergy away from the congregation; or stone screen and pulpits might separate the audience from those officiating, as in the sixth-century *schola cantorum* placed in the rebuilt twelfth-century church of San Clemente (Figure 6). Such elaborations are also to be found in the screens of Gothic churches, or the raised chancel of Romanesque churches (Figure 7).

104   The basilican form of church was of immense importance for mediaeval art. You can see almost every mediaeval church pattern as an elaboration of this simple hall form. Romanesque added tiers of small, round-topped windows in the apse. Gothic builders pierced the walls of aisles and apse with huge windows. Romanesque architects added tall towers to the façade and/or over the crossing. Gothic artists decorated exteriors and interiors with such an elegant fantasy of painted tracery, pinnacles and, later, fan-vaulting that the simple nave, aisles, hall structure is almost (but not quite) submerged. Now it is true that an idea of the central-plan church was always present – square, octagon, Greek cross, circle and their combinations. Its greatest and most important example was the church of the Holy Sepulchre in Jerusalem. This idea delighted late fifteenth- and early sixteenth-century artists; it was a continuous theme of many mediaeval baptistry and early mediaeval tomb structures (Figure 8); it may well go back to the round Etruscan tombs of Italy taken over by pagan Rome,

and may have been connected with baptismal buildings through the Pauline doctrine of baptism as the death of sin and rejuvenation by faith, for, of course, centrally planned Roman temples were not then an acceptable precedent. But it remained in the middle ages a 'minority' form of religious ground plan.

105   As one gazes down the nave of Santa Sabina, one is not a bit surprised to see a diminishing perspective of arches bouncing their curving lines away. But putting arches over columns was an innovation of Christian architects in the Late Empire. They *did* follow classical canons in putting a flat architrave over columns in some churches (Figure 9) but it was the innovation which 'won' artistically. The squat columns supporting heavy rounded arches of Romanesque, the grouped columns carrying pointed arches in Gothic, the transformation of capitals in Romanesque and Byzantine architecture into more solid, less undercut forms than those of the classical orders, and their often virtual disappearance as separate components in the soaring piers of Gothic, stem (however remotely) from this decision.

106   The columns of Santa Sabina are Corinthian ones – almost certainly made newly and especially for the church. You will not find this in the church of S. Cecilia in Trastevere in Rome (Figure 10) where the Romanesque architects remodelled the façade (note the *flat* architrave which had not disappeared) using late-antique columns of African marble of different colours and different forms. Between the period of Santa Sabina, and the remodelling of S. Cecilia in Trastevere, Rome's population had dwindled, her trade had virtually ceased and her links with the sources of new architectural raw materials had weakened. Building materials were looted from Roman pagan buildings or kept carefully from old structures which architects rebuilt. In northern Europe and in other areas of Italy with no huge quantity of ruins to loot or copy, and no Mediterranean marble to import, the classical orders were forgotten, except in the odd, unillustrated manuscript of Vitruvius (the Roman writer on architecture) in a monastic library. Even in Rome, where craftsmen were sitting on top of piles of concrete examples of that style, classical examples were lost. Elsewhere there was an even deeper gulf. Texts were not much use. Abbot Suger used a Vitruvius but he built what has been called the first Gothic church (Figure 11).

107   Why were the ideas of Christian artists and patrons so important in shaping mediaeval art – indeed in many more ways than I have described? While it is true that when barbarians invaded Europe from the north, the indigenous population had not been members of the 'civilized' world for long, and when Arab armies invaded the Mediterranean territories of the Roman Empire they represented a sophisticated rival culture, nevertheless the old pattern of the Late Empire was shattered, trade links were cut and old boundaries disappeared. Almost everywhere the only institutions which remained at all stable were those of the church (and especially their new religious strongholds, the monasteries) which often took over many of the political, social or even military functions of Imperial administration who continued to issue orders from the safety of Constantinople but without rendering ultimately effective assistance. Arab invasions wiped out the once powerful Christian communities of North Africa and Asia Minor which had rivalled the Church of Rome (St. Augustine had been the product of this Mediterranean Church). This was the situation: that Christian ideas of what was acceptable in pagan art and culture came to dominate what intellectual life and artistic energy was left in Europe; that the Bishop of Rome gradually approached a position where he was *de facto* the leader of religion in the western Empire – the *Pope;* that through the ineffectiveness and beleaguered isolation of Constantinople, Byzantine art began to diverge from what had been originally (a style like that of Rome) an early Christian adaptation of pagan artistic styles; and that an independent *western*

Christendom with independent artistic forms emerged. One of the major historical themes of the Middle Ages was to be the struggle of the Bishop of Rome to assert his independence of the Patriarch of Constantinople (ending with the schism between eastern and western Christianity in the mid-eleventh century) and his even longer struggle to assert spiritual and temporal authority over the heirs of barbarian invasions – and the feudal alliances and later, emergent nation-states – of western Europe. It is against this political background that we should see the story of the varied contacts in mediaeval art between the styles of native 'barbarians', Rome, and Byzantium.

108   Between the fifth and eighth centuries many of the forms and functions of Roman and Greek art simply became irrelevant. Triumphal arches and portraits of victorious generals or reliefs showing their campaigns obviously had no place. Roman baths fell into disuse when aqueducts were pulled down by besieging armies and the vast water supplies needed for their existence were cut off. It was a society which needed fortification not palaces; temporary wooden structures, towers and massive walls rather than country villas or elegant public parks dotted about with antique statuary. It was a society which became defensive, temporary – at least in its concept of worldly existence, and orientated more and more towards rural subsistence rather than luxurious urban culture. The Christian ethos had no direct use for the forms of pagan gods or temples. Old techniques often could not be practised (mosaic, bronze, marble, brick work) as trade links withered and industry was dislocated. Craftsmen who held the traditions of antique art in their hands and heads no longer travelled all over Europe. Patronage which in more peaceful times had a wide social representation shrank to a narrow spectrum of church and monastic requirements. And by the time Europe had somewhat recovered, as you will gather from Units 3–4, a society had emerged with very different characteristics from those of the late Roman Imperial society.

109   Yet the 'Dark Ages' (so-called because so little verbal or visual evidence *illuminates* them) was really a very productive period. Looking at two Gospel illustrations produced in northern Europe at this time (Figures 12–13), can you suggest why I should think this?

Just because they *were* isolated from their old cultural links, Irish and Saxon illuminators were able to add bold and often very beautiful 'grafts' of native culture to the memory of early Christian Mediterranean forms. The early Christian visual symbol for an evangelist is an image of the power and strength of an animal rather than an identifiable creature (one you could name) in an instant of action. At Lindisfarne a monk has copied an earlier illustration too. Like the Irish designer he makes complex patterns out of the components of an originally quite 'realistic' picture: even the calligraphy, while readable, turns the rounded forms of Roman lettering into a more jagged and less regular geometry. When the design experiments produced by such isolated little cultures were injected into the mainstream of European art (after a meander of several centuries) they had a vital effect.

110   Two of the factors contributing to mediaeval art have already been explained: the maintenance of one type of Early Christian adaptation of classical styles in the relatively stable area of Rome, and the interesting variations of it produced in isolated communities in northern Europe. The third main factor was also one produced by isolation – the special brand of design which was produced in Constantinople and which came to be called Byzantine art. Why was this style important? Many Popes were Greeks and members of the papal court too were Greeks. Its true that Byzantium didn't hold northern Italy for

long. The Goths invaded in the fifth century and the Lombards in the sixth. At this period Ravenna was the seat of the Byzantine Emperor's representative (the Exarch) and at Ravenna magnificent buildings and mosaics, which were to impress and influence mediaeval artists, were commissioned (Figure 8). Even though Byzantium lost control of this area, it maintained commercial links with Venice. In the south of Italy it was only ousted by the Normans in the late eleventh century, and still left enough Greek-speaking communities for Petrarch to try to learn Greek from a southern Italian in the fourteenth century. The sheer fact that the Byzantine Empire retained enough stability to possess an efficient administration, army and navy meant that it retained artistic expertise (with continuous links with antiquity) which was frequently sought by western Europeans, though there was a period of iconoclasm in the eighth century, when virtually no figurative religious representations were allowed. Yet Byzantine styles were very impressive to Western artists serving the gradually diverging concepts of Christianity. Even iconoclasm had a spin-off effect, for craftsmen may have moved to Rome to make the brilliant figurative mosaics of the early ninth century (Figure 14). Even after the schism (the final doctrinal break between Constantinople and Rome) the Abbot of Monte Cassino used Byzantine craftsmen to help him rebuild his church and to train monks in mosaic techniques – as you will read in one of the documents I deal with in Section 3. It is probable that Abbot Desiderius' trained monks made the apse decoration of San Clemente in Rome, around 1200 (Figure 15). Just to show how complicated the question of Byzantine influence is – the mosaic's closest parallel is a fifth- or sixth-century Byzantine mosaic design at Ravenna. It is a mosaic representing the rood as the tree of life. In the centre there's the stark shape of the cross with an emaciated Christ and thin little figures of St. John and the Virgin. From the same source as the cross, and surrounding it, grow the ebullient acanthus scrolls of the tree of life, and the bony branches of the tree of thorns which are entwined on the cross. Into this broad design are inserted tiny little scenes from the lives of saints and figures of the doctors of the church, while above them are little pagan deities, embraced as it were by the Church. In Sicily too at this period, the Normans, who had ousted Byzantium politically, created churches and palaces which are stylistic-ally still part of the Byzantine Empire (Figure 16). Sicilian (Pisan too – as I'll explain later) decorations at this time are also influenced by Arab art and it is worth stressing that the northern barbarian and southern Arabian invasions of Europe were quite different in impact in that the latter actually represented a sophisticated rival culture (in art, a *non*-figurative emphasis however) to that of Europe.

(ii) Pan-European styles: Carolingian, Ottonian, Romanesque and Gothic

111   Byzantine and Roman art of the Late Imperial period particularly impressed Carolingian artists. The style of the latter centred on Aachen in the early ninth century and was based on the power of Charlemagne – the leader of the Franks – who created a brief but still important European peace in alliance with the Pope, and became the first Holy Roman Emperor. Carolingian art is often represented as a 'renaissance' – the first important attempt to create a 'second Rome' in northern Europe. If you compare an ivory book cover made at Metz in the late ninth century with the fourth-century wooden doors of Santa Sabina (Figures 17 and 4, 5) you can see how well Carolingian artists were able to recreate the styles of late classical antiquity. Yet another ivory book cover, executed at the Irish foundation of the monastery of St. Gall (Figure 18),

shows however that within Carolingian art there were more 'native' facets: in particular (as when the legend is of St. Gall being fed by animals) where a story had to be represented for which there were not exact earlier models. In these scenes of enormous creatures feeding monks (the tiny trees have huge leaves and small branches), as so often in the *detail* of mediaeval art there is a marvellous sense of humour – and *good*-humoured humour at that. This sense of fun, sadly enough, is not really to be found in 'Renaissance' art or its followers, when a very self-conscious concept of the professional dignity of art took over – except perhaps in the naughty cherubs of Donatello and Raphael. More seriously, I would stress that Carolingian art gained as much vitality from its enthusiastic copying of earlier forms, as from its own 'native' barbaric presentation of themes. To stress its debt to northern Europe: while Rome's libraries *were* ransacked for 'authentic' texts, many texts copied by Carolingian *scriptoria* are actually Irish ones, *themselves* copied from late Antique texts.

112   The Carolingian Empire lasted only half a century. It was disrupted by the last major wave of European invasions: Arabs in the south, Norsemen, and Hungarians in the east. But in the late tenth and eleventh centuries the Saxon dynasty of the Ottonians managed to unify a large part of Europe, taking the title of Holy Roman Emperor again and copying the Carolingian 'renaissance' of art and culture. Ottonian art merged into the first truly pan-European mediaeval style: Romanesque, which as its name implies, means a style following 'Roman' models. On this side of the Channel it is called 'Norman' architecture. In its style buildings are massive and fortress-like. Round arches rest on strong columns. Roofing is barrel-vaulted. Thick walls of halls, apses and towers are pierced with regular rows or tiers of small round arched windows, or decorative blind arches. Inside, the simple walls of the basilican nave are elaborated in tiers of arcades held together vertically by piers from floor to ceiling. Despite the great height of these buildings, as at Speyer or Durham (Figures 19–20), the effect is still very ground-clinging and ponderous. Sculptural ornament of architecture (Figure 20) is boldly geometrical or consists of stylized animal patterns, which had been a feature of 'barbarian' art since the Romano-Celtic period. Figured sculpture is massive and very little undercut, clinging to the surfaces of walls in low relief and often, as in Wiligelmo's sculpture of the killing of Cain in Modena (Figure 21), with a bold simplicity which is very impressive especially when you consider that low relief in fifteenth-century Italy was so often used (except by Donatello) for delicate detail – subtle and pretty effects. In this building style there's plenty of space for murals and these, like the one representing the lives of St. Clement and St. Alexis in the lower church of San Clemente in Rome (Figure 22), and like earlier Roman mosaics and contemporary sculpture, use heavy outline, simple forms, sweeping draperies, huge-eyed faces and very bold effects. Manuscript illumination is similarly abstract and decorative. Just as murals and sculpture cling closely to the shape of the building or harmonize with its forms, manuscript illuminations have a strong affinity with the abstract rhythms of the accompanying calligraphy.

113   In the mid-twelfth century in France this style began to be replaced by what was to be an equally pan-European style, though much more independent of late Roman and Byzantine forms. Gothic buildings are more vertical in emphasis, and stress delicacy and lightness. Thinner walls and larger windows are possible because most of the weight of the building is taken by huge grouped columns and buttresses. Windows are filled with stained glass and this ousts mural decoration. Arches and vaults are pointed or sometimes 'onion-shaped'

(ogival), and ribs of stone create complex webs of tracery. Pointed pinnacles, transparent 'bird-cage' towers, façades covered in elongated figure sculpture give a very graceful, sometimes finicky effect. At a distance, a cathedral like that of Rheims (1230) looks like a fragile piece of coral, brittle and insubstantial (Figure 23). This delicacy and slenderness of form, this love of minute pattern is found in contemporary sculpture and manuscript illumination (Figures 24–25). The latter media also show a love of the sinuous curve and a sense of pliable forms – which, naturally, buildings don't display. Free standing figures (though small ones) begin to appear (Figure 24). Iconographical schemes become more and more complex, especially on façades, and rather than the awesome Last Judgements and starkly presented events of the Old Testament a choice of more gentle and intimate scenes is apparent (Figures 22 and 25).

Now, without looking back, summarize in note form what happened in European art during the thousand years after the first successful barbarian invasion of the Roman Empire.

Invasion brought social and trade disruption, and the isolation of cultures, but it increased the power of the Church, as well as breaking up the unity of the Mediterranean world. Christian needs and ethics dictated what pagan forms should be retained or adapted. Isolation created a situation where native artistic idiosyncrasies flourished without contact with the old Mediterranean centres. The art of Constantinople remained an important influence but diverged gradually from the styles of the new western Christendom, now looking to Rome for spiritual leadership. When a relatively peaceful Europe emerged, the idiosyncratic artistic styles merged into the pan-European styles of first Romanesque, and then Gothic (both centring on northern Europe: the new power base). While these styles still maintained many traditions reaching back to the Christian adaptations of pagan classical forms (the basilica, the representation of the authors of the gospel, the acanthus scroll ornament, etc.) the forms they took look so different from their precedents that they seem to have little connection with them. It is in this context that I now want to look at the work of Italian artists, especially Tuscans in the later Middle Ages.

2   MEDIAEVAL ITALIAN AND, IN PARTICULAR, TUSCAN ART

114   What was Italian art like during the Middle Ages? It was in rather an odd position. Because Italy was the heartland of Early Christian artistic traditions, possessed Rome, the seat of the Papacy, and perhaps because it was the easiest source of access to Byzantine styles, it was a continuous influence on northern Europe. But as Italy itself tended to adopt transalpine artistic ideas slowly and selectively it was rather a 'backwater' – still building in brick and marble, altering basilican church forms very little, and decorating the simple hall shape with mosaic and murals. To give an example: the first Italian-made stained glass window with a figurative design is in Siena Cathedral, and is dated 1288. Now I've used the phrase 'Italian art' but this is hardly suitable to describe the very heterogeneous provincial styles existing in the peninsula either in the 'early Renaissance' or 'mediaeval' period. Rome was always an artistic centre which was a law unto itself. For instance, it produced virtually no sculpture for a thousand years. Architecturally, it could rest content with

the huge Constantinian basilicas, whereas other areas in Italy needed many new church buildings. It is typical that there are few remotely 'Gothic' churches in Rome – Santa Maria Sopra Minerva is one – and that for the most part Rome reflects Gothic and Romanesque styles in items like tombs, altar canopies (ciboria) or additions to church fabrics like Romanesque towers. You can see the sort of 'extraneous' role these northern European styles took in the interior and on the exterior of Santa Cecilia in Trastevere (Figure 26). Southern Italy was less independent – it was always under some alien power: first Byzantium, then the Normans, then Hohenstaufen and finally the Angevins. The influence of their rulers is reflected in Sicilian buildings of the eleventh and twelfth centuries, and in quite numerous Gothic monuments in Naples. Northern Italy was often invaded by northern European powers, but it was never forced into single unified territories for long like the south. In the later Middle Ages, northern Italian towns began to organize themselves into independent Republican communes or small city-centred dukedoms: the city states which were to play such an important part in the 'early Renaissance'. They adapted Romanesque and Gothic styles to their particular needs. Indeed they were not just on the receiving end artistically, as Lombard builders played an important part in originating Romanesque forms. It was natural that northern and southern Italy should respond more wholeheartedly to Romanesque and Gothic, than Rome. Particularly in northern Italy, the period of urban growth and consequent demand for church, palace and town hall building, for decorating buildings and making elaborate tombs, coincided with the period of Romanesque and Gothic in northern Europe. Venice formed something of an exception in the north: not because it didn't organize itself as a city state, but because its commercial contacts with the eastern Mediterranean made it especially close to Byzantine influences. Yet even this rather neat division of the peninsula hides a great deal of complex interaction. For instance, Venetian mosaicists were called in to decorate the Florentine baptistry in a thoroughly Byzantine manner (Figure 27). Tuscan painters worked in Rome in the later Middle Ages too, and Tuscan sculptors in Naples.

115   What had happened to Tuscan art in the Middle Ages? Even in the fifteenth century there was not much trace of art and architecture dating from the fifth to the tenth century. The area had been as effectively devastated as parts of northern Europe. The Goths invaded in the fifth century. The Byzantine Emperor reconquered the area only to be faced by another successful invasion by barbarians in the sixth century: this time, the Lombards. Between the sixth and eighth century the Lombards established a dukedom based at Lucca, though the Byzantine Empire hung on to coastal areas for some time. In the late eighth century the Franks invaded Italy at the request of the Pope and among other areas took over Tuscany, making it part of the Carolingian Empire. These Frankish counts (based again at Lucca) held the area against Arab pirates, and dominated the Lombardo-Gothic population. They were succeeded in the mid-eleventh century by a native family. During this period Tuscany seems to have been a very chaotic area: the valley of the Arno was covered in marshes, the mountains were uncultivated refuges for practically pagan communities, and areas close to towns were preyed upon by Frankish feudal lords. Traces survive of early basilicas (usually mentioned in guide books as vague 'foundations' beneath a building). At the end of the period there is the odd, tiny parish church crudely constructed from huge rough blocks of stone and containing massively simple 'native Lombard' sculpture – not unlike Celtic churches (Figure 28). There are virtually no paintings. Indeed, it is highly significant that it took an Irish missionary in the sixth century to encourage the Luccans to begin a building programme which had produced twenty-two churches in their tiny town by the fifteenth century. San Frediano,

as the Tuscans call him, is thought to have come from Ulster. Typical of the dearth of evidence at this period, he can only be identified tentatively.

116 It was really in the eleventh century that a society made up of the descendants of Etruscans, Latins, Goths, Lombards and Franks began to emerge in Tuscany, which we can call 'Italian'. Note that although this area was once in the heartland of the Roman Empire, it was not very much more 'Roman' by the eleventh century than the Anglo-Saxon, Celtic, Norse (with Norman rulers) community which finally turned into England. This is worth saying, because all discussions of the Italian Renaissance tempt one only too easily to think that classicism was somehow 'in the blood' of Tuscans, and only needed to be 'tapped'. In this new society, industrial and commercial activity was initiated. Pisa, Pistoia, Lucca and Florence gained independence as communally organized city states. They benefited from the war between the Ottonian Empire and the Papacy, in which both sides were so eager for support that they gave concessions to allies. The countryside began to show more prosperity. The reclamation and more intensive use of land was encouraged by a proliferation of many small property-holdings. There was a good deal of competitiveness between the cities. Pisa took over from Lucca in dominating the area until the late thirteenth century because of its favourable position at the mouth of the Arno. Then, gradually, Florence began to take over and by the early fifteenth century had conquered Pisa.

117 Tuscan art and architecture really 'begins' in the eleventh century. It was this art and architecture – what is called Lombard Romanesque – that dominated the landscape for a fifteenth-century Tuscan artist, and it was a product of Siena, Orvieto, Arezzo, the cities (Pistoia, Lucca, Prato) around Pisa, Pisa itself, as well as Florence. You will find that the first pair of baptistry doors for Florence were made by Pisan workmen. It was a point of pride that the second and third pair were made by Florentines. In other words, Florentine artistic self-assertion in the fifteenth century is *very* much a counterpart to a political movement. In this example, Florence was asserting herself as the leading city of Tuscany. To take another one: the mosaics inside the Florentine Baptistry were begun by Venetian and Roman artists (Figure 27). They were completed by native workmen. Here Florence is asserting her artistic independence of the rest of Italy too.

118 What sort of architecture did fourteenth- and fifteenth-century Tuscan artists see around them? Was it 'Gothic' or 'Romanesque'. Try to decide this by looking at these buildings (Figures 29–39, 19–20, 23).

At Pisa they would have seen a cathedral founded in 1063, consecrated in 1118 and completed in the fourteenth century, a separate cylindrical bell tower built between the late twelfth and the late fourteenth century, and a circular baptistry finished at the same time as the tower but begun a little earlier (Figure 29). This magnificent architectural complex (certainly the envy of Florence) comprises a great heterogeneity of styles, mainly because its erection took so long to complete. The granite columns of the baptistry come from Roman temples in Sardinia and Elba. Such re-utilization of classical material was common in Romanesque forms. Roman gravestones were inserted into the walls of the Cathedral, which is faced with marble. Both these features are Byzantine. The dome has an Islamic 'onion-shaped' outline. The apse and façade decoration of blind arches on the cathedral and the tiers of little arches on the bell-tower remind one of the northern European example of Speyer, yet it is a Tuscan version of Romanesque, with a *separate* bell tower. This Tuscan (Italian actually) custom meant that bell towers don't form an integral part of the shape of the body of the church as they do in northern Europe, where there may be as many as seven towers over entrances or crossings, in both Gothic and Romanesque churches. The Gothic elements in this Pisan building complex are really matters of detail: of decoration. You can see this in the upper part of the façade of the baptistry and the spiky decoration of the drum of the dome. The status of Gothic forms in Pisan architecture as a whole is similar. There is one very Gothic church in Pisa – the Church of Santa Maria della Spina, but it is a very small building – almost a Pisan religious 'folly' (Figure 30). The churches of Lucca and Pistoia represent the same stylistic 'balance', with Romanesque essentials and Gothic additions. A view of Lucca cathedral, for instance, shows similar characteristics to that of Pisa, though without such complex arcading in the apse and, of course, without the dome (Figure 31). In this case, the Gothic stylistic addition is in the interior modelling of the cathedral, carried out in the fourteenth and fifteenth centuries. The building was founded by San Frediano in the sixth century and rebuilt in the same time span as Pisa cathedral – between 1060 and the late thirteenth century. Churches at Pistoia too show tiers of rows of round-arched arcades and bold 'zebra-striped' marble facing. Sometimes façades are varied, with elaborate sculpture and figured marbles (abstract animal designs) as at the Luccan church of San Michele, or the columns of the arcades have different designs – they are decorated with mosaic, twisted, knotted, fluted, or topped by grotesquely carved capitals. This means that although Tuscan Romanesque appears more neat and simple in shape than the Gothic, it has complex and varied detail of pattern. Florence, though not so active architecturally as towns lower in the Arno valley between the eleventh and thirteenth century, also displayed Romanesque styles. But at Ss. Apostoli, San Miniato and San Giovanni it is apparent that Florentines adopted a much less decorated, much more severe type of design. San Miniato for instance, rebuilt between 1018 and 1220 in Florence, has the typical 'zebra-striped' exterior of Pisan buildings, but no intricate architectural ornament at all (Figure 34). The Florentine baptistry which was remodelled between 1050 and 1228 on an earlier sixth or seventh century structure has an affinity with the baptistry at Pistoia (Figure 35), but is much less elaborate than the Pisan baptistry. I would like to remind you here that the central plan baptistry design originated in the period of the Late Empire and just afterwards.

119   The most extreme versions of Gothic style in Tuscany were to be found in Siena, and in Orvieto – both south of the towns in the Arno of which we have been talking and both in the mountains (Figures 36, 37). The façade of Orvieto was designed by Lorenzo Maitani (a Sienese) between 1308 and 1330, and that of Siena (the lower half at any rate) by Giovanni Pisano (from Pisa – naturally) between 1285 and 1295. To give you an idea of how long it took 'Gothic' to reach Tuscan architecture: the first Gothic building – the Abbey of St Denis – was erected in the mid-twelfth century. I want you now to compare the façade of Orvieto, the lower half of the façade of Siena, and those of the cathedrals of Rheims (built 1230s) and Laon (built 1190–1200) (Figures 36–38, 23).

Both Italian façades are flatter than their French counterparts. They don't have such deep embrasures for windows or doors, nor such heavy and emphatic buttresses. At Siena and Laon all three doors have a rounded arch. At Orvieto the central door has a rounded arch, while at Rheims all doors have steeply pointed arches with echoing arches above them. In other words, the two Italian examples followed more old-fashioned Gothic principles in their use of rounded arches. Now, while the façades of Orvieto and Siena use more figure sculpture than previous Tuscan examples, they still do not display the myriad statues in niches which cover both French façades. Typically, both Tuscan examples use mosaic panels as centre-pieces and this was an ancient custom in Italy. The Romanesque church of San Frediano in Lucca does this, as do earlier churches in Rome. And even though the Tuscan 'gothic' façades adapt decoration with figure sculpture, Giovanni Pisano at Siena did not put his figures at the sides of his doors as a French architect would have done, but between the arches of the doors above the door frames. Without the tall flanking towers of the French façades too, the Tuscan designs still possess the stable, horizontal effect of Romanesque. Fifteenth-century Florentine artists would have been able to see church interiors too, modelled on Gothic lines especially at Santa Croce, and S. Maria Novella, but here the rule is similar – that Tuscans produced their own rather conservative version of French styles.

120   The story of Tuscan sculpture, and to a lesser extent painting, is a variation of that of architecture. It is a variation because while there are a lot of Romanesque buildings in Tuscany, and not many Gothic ones, the situation is the opposite in the former media. Can you think of a very simple reason for this?

Such media (except for small church utensils, the odd private commission and the illuminated manuscript) were always conceived of as decorating a building – a mural for a wall, a sculpture to decorate a façade, a tomb or pulpit, an altarpiece – and the first phase of artistic activity in Tuscany was occupied with building churches and town halls. Hence you go to see Gothic sculpture in Romanesque buildings, or ones completed only in the Gothic period but begun much earlier, and to see 'early Renaissance' murals in Gothic structures – or since Florentines (perhaps because they were so argumentative: Vasari would surely say, so *keen* to have the *best*) had a bad habit of not completing façades, in churches with very battered and rough exteriors. Speaking of heterogeneity, and incidentally what Italians are pleased to call 'Gothic', have a look at the interior of S. Francesco in Arezzo (Figure 39). It was built in 1290 in the very sober form of Gothic approved by Franciscans. It is in the altar chapel of this church that Piero della Francesca, the great fifteenth-century painter, made his frescos.

121   What was Tuscan sculpture like at this period? First I want you to compare a pulpit made by Nicola Pisano between 1259 and 1260 for the baptistry at Pisa, and a relief made for Strasbourg Cathedral thirty years earlier (Figures 40–42), then compare Pisano's work with the Gothic, Romanesque and early Christian sculptures we have already examined (Figures 4–5, 17–18, 21, 24).

Nicola Pisano's relief shows the same crisp detail, varied composition and modelling of drapery falling in 'V' folds that is displayed in the Strasbourg relief. Yet his composition is calm beside the tense emotion (almost bordering on the grotesque in its exaggerated reactions) of the Strasbourg scene. Pisano's relief is also quite stolid and 'down to earth' in comparison with the sinuous elegance and 'sweet' charm of the little gilt statuette of the Virgin and Child. These differences link Pisano closely with the way Wiligelmo's figures seem to cling to the block of stone, or even to the rounded chubby forms modelled on the wooden doors of Santa Sabina. In other words, Pisano was clearly keen to adopt the French manner of composing varied narrative scenes and the precise techniques of modelling shapes, but, like Tuscan architects adapting Gothic designs, he still clung to older Romanesque and pre-Romanesque conventions. His figures have a sturdy strength that reminds one of the ponderous curves of many Roman Imperial reliefs. Indeed, the hairstyle of the Virgin, the snorting horses' heads and the facial profiles of his figures suggest he had studied classical examples. Pisano founded the most important school of Tuscan sculpture until the advent of the Florentines in the fifteenth century. His son Giovanni designed the lower façade of Siena Cathedral. Andrea Pisano designed the first pair of bronze doors for the Florentine baptistry between 1330 and 1336 (Figure 43). His pupils Tino da Camaino of Siena and Arnolfo di Cambio (probably a Florentine) carried Pisan ideas to, respectively, Naples and Rome from their native Tuscany (Figure 44). Looking at these illustrations (Figures 24, 42–44), did Pisano's heirs maintain his attitude to Gothic designs?

Giovanni and Andrea Pisano clearly did adopt that elegant elongation of figures and slender sharpness of design which Nicola had not really adopted, though they certainly did not ever quite catch the hysteria of emotional reaction present in the Strasbourg narrative. When you come to study fifteenth-century sculpture in Unit 8, you will find that Lorenzo Ghiberti is the true heir to the Gothic-Tuscan tradition of polish and precision, although he does explore even *more* varied composition (graduation of relief from high to low, landscape detail, many figures) through his interest in perspective. However, Tino da Camaino and Arnolfo di Cambio, while they adopted Gothic forms *more* wholeheartedly than had Nicola, nevertheless retain something of that ponderous monumentality of form, that sense of calmness, which has direct links with Romanesque and Late Imperial Roman styles. This strand in late mediaeval Tuscan sculpture is, I believe, taken up by Donatello, and harmonized with fifteenth-century interest in learning directly from Early Roman Imperial sculptures.

122 Gothic architects in northern Europe had decorated their buildings largely with figure sculpture and stained glass. They do not seem to have been interested in mosaic, and while there *were* murals painted at the period few have survived, and those that *have* done so are not very impressive. The main employment of painting was in illumination of manuscripts, and in the colouring of architecture and sculpture. So, whereas Tuscan sculptors and architects could clearly learn a good deal from their French counterparts in an easy and obvious manner, Tuscan painters tended to cling to established native traditions (especially those of Venice or Rome) rather than translate small-scale designs from contemporary French manuscripts to larger-scale panels and walls. And while they seem to have been influenced by French sculptural experiments in composition, this meant translating a three-dimensional medium into two dimensions. The influence of Gothic sculpture *may* help to explain the very 'volumetric' quality especially noticeable in Giotto's work in the early fifteenth century and in the work of panel painters like Duccio (Figures 45, 46, 51). It should not be forgotten, of course, that the examples of sculptures seen would all be vividly coloured, thus making the 'translation' easier, perhaps, to conceive.

Looking at a church interior painted by Giotto, it may be hard to see him as part of the city of Rome's tradition of mural and mosaic decoration – to think of his work as linked with the apse of San Clemente for instance (Figure 15). The link is a very simple one. Giotto and the mosaicists of San Clemente make mural decorations which actually take into account the structural shapes they decorate: they both think 'big' and think architecturally. They consider *general* symmetry of disposition, as well as the particular composition of individual scenes. Gothic artists did this with a sculptured façade or a stained glass window, but not with murals, when they tended to pile little scenes on top of one another without regard for the whole effect. There is a third possible factor at work in Tuscan painting of the thirteenth and fourteenth centuries, especially the work of Giotto: the influence of non-Italian Byzantine art. At this period especially in Yugoslavia, mosaicists were producing what can only be called Giottoesque narratives (Figures 46, 47). No one has yet been able to explain this satisfactorily. It may of course mean that there was an *incipient* naturalism present in Byzantine art which developed at the same time but independently in Eastern Europe and Italy *without* actual contacts between the styles. It is for these reasons, since Tuscan sculptors and architects had, as it were, direct counterparts in northern Europe, and Italian painters did *not*, that the history of Tuscan mural painting at this period is rather 'eccentric' in its connections. This eccentricity may help to explain the unprecedented importance painting was to have in following centuries in Italy – as a particularly experimental medium.

beginning

irregular; odd; whimsical.

123 Giotto's mural style is to be 'explained' mainly in terms of a tradition of mosaic work in Rome: with the mosaics made by Jacopo Torriti and Pietro Cavallini in the thirteenth century (Figure 9). Both artists were probably led to take a careful look at the styles of late Imperial mosaic work through being given the job of repairing some examples in Roman churches. But like Nicola Pisano's work, Giotto's work was interpreted in a more Gothic manner by his pupils (Figures 48–49). Taddeo Gaddi's little narrative shows a closer affinity with French styles than Giotto's paintings. Nevertheless it is a 'compromise' style. In comparison with the French narrative (Figures 48–49) his figures are weightier and rounder in form, the textures bolder and simpler in contrast (cloudlets and pinnacles in the French narrative's sky, cobbled paving, fantastic costume details to compare with a pure blue sky, plain 'floor', simple drapery shapes in Gaddi's version). In particular I noticed a contrast between the treatment of the group around the priest (at the top of the flight of steps in both cases). The figures in Gaddi's scene simply *do not* undulate as the French illuminations do. Gaddi, like Nicola Pisano, emphasizes the sturdy and stocky in form, not the precious and finicky.

And Tuscan altarpieces more than murals, especially in Siena, translated the Gothic formula quite wholeheartedly. Duccio and Simone Martini, in the late thirteenth and early fourteenth centuries, represent in their elegant reserve something very much closer in mood to French styles (Figures 50–51). In particular, the rear face of Duccio's altarpiece (Figure 51) reminds one of Andrea Pisano's treatment of the scenes in the slightly later Baptistry doors of Florence (Figure 43). This difference in reception to Gothic styles between murals and panels may be explained by the closer relationship in scale between French manuscript illustrations and Tuscan altarpieces – and the portable nature of the altarpiece.

One thinks loosely of 'Renaissance' taking over from Gothic. This is not really the way to look at what happened in Italy. Perhaps you will remember that Vasari in his *Lives of the Artists* describes the 'rebirth' of art as a rejection of Byzantine and barbarian styles: which he describes as 'maniera greca' and 'gothic' respectively – the latter simply meaning 'barbarian' or Romanesque to us. While Gothic art did have *some* impact on Tuscany, quite a lot in south Italy and very little in Rome, it did not transform the whole cultural and physical landscape as it did in the north of Europe. Now fifteenth-century Florentines clearly see themselves as rejecting 'the Greek manner', Romanesque and, to a lesser extent, Gothic modes. In fact, by mistake they sometimes copied Romanesque ideas because they thought they were actually classical; for instance, they thought their Baptistry *classical* (Figure 35). Without knowing

It, too, they may have developed the incipient realism in late Gothic and late Byzantine art to create 'early Renaissance' naturalism. Having said that fifteenth-century Florentine artists may well have created a new style on the basis of some borrowing from apparently hostile styles, it is also true, I think, that the contemporary use of classical sculpture and classical architectural texts was also made possible by the sheer fact that Italy had for so long remained an artistic backwater, and had clung to Late Antique modes.

3 COMPARISON AND CONTRAST BETWEEN MEDIAEVAL AND RENAISSANCE ART: AN INTRODUCTION TO THE DEBATE OF UNITS 8–13

You will need the set book: Elizabeth G. Holt (ed) (1957) *A Documentary History of Art*, Volume I Doubleday & Co., New York, 1957–8.

124 This section is no more than a very general and rather selective view of the comparison between mediaeval and Renaissance art, which we deal with in greater detail in Units 8–13. The debate about the differences between the two styles and whether there really *is* a wide divide separating them covers many topics. Do they use fundamentally different techniques (Units 8–9 and television programme 07)? What are their views of artistic status (Units 12 and 13) and the role of art (Units 10, 11 and 12)? Do they emphasize different types of subject-matter (Unit 11 and radio programme 11)? Is the personnel of art, as well as subject-matter and function more secular (Units 12, 11 and 8)? Do they differ in their attitude to classical forms and ideas on art (Units 9 and 10)? Are they more interested in realism (Unit 10)? Is their pattern of patronage different (Unit 12 and radio programme 12)? Are they poles apart in their view of the individual (Units 10 and 12)? I intend that through reading many of the mediaeval documents in Section I of the set book you will gain an intimate idea of mediaeval artists' and patrons' attitude to these topics, to set against the course units' stronger emphasis on fifteenth-century events and ideas.

(i) Individualism and Secularization

125 Before reading particular documents, look at the contents pages of the set book (pp. xi–xvii) and make notes on the way the sort of information provided on the Renaissance (Section 2) differs from that on the Middle Ages (Section 1).

The Renaissance documents largely consist of accounts by artists of their own work (Ghiberti, Alberti, Filarete, della Francesca, Leonardo, Dürer) biographies of individual artists (Manetti, Van Mander, Van Sandrart) or short descriptions of individuals' styles and value (Fazio). There are letters by and to artists, contracts for paintings and a report on the archaeology of classical Rome for a Pope. The mediaeval documents have a very different character. Two artists write on art (de Honnecourt, Cennini) and two describe their work's *content* (Paris and Pucelle). There are no letters, except from clerics, and some contracts – but only for large building works. One monk who probably wasn't an artist writes a treatise on art. There are accounts of 'foreign' art (Constantinople, the Holy Land) but not a very archaeological attitude when it comes to the marvels of Rome. Most documents tell how individual churches were built, from the standpoint of the monastic patron. There is some material on the legal position of artists (guild regulations). Most of the authors are clerics, not laymen and there is very little interest in the individual artist. Before accepting that Renaissance art differed from mediaeval in that it was more secular and individualistic, I would like to make some points.

126   There's very little written evidence about anyone (except the highest clerics and princes) in the Middle Ages, so people may well have praised individuality but simply reserved writing to essential matters like law, administration, war and theology. I would stress how much evidence may have disappeared during centuries of accidents, social disruption and invasion. You have to remember that, during the fifteenth century, printing was invented, multiplying copies of books giving information about artists, by artists, so that it was very difficult for information to disappear – as it so easily might do in the case of a book available only in a few manuscript copies. Without printed evidence, we would find it very difficult to deduce much about the individuality of most fifteenth- and sixteenth-century Italian artists. Most Renaissance artists only signed their work sporadically, for instance.

127   It is often said that during the Middle Ages art was intended to embellish the institutions of church and monarchy for the greater glory of God, and artists were simply considered humble agents, not creators of works. Nevertheless, we have got to stress that the number of laymen writing about art, patronizing it and being artists, and the interest in individuality, increase in the later Middle Ages, and do not abruptly appear in fifteenth-century Florence. Of course, you could argue that this is no more than the result of the fact that during the later Middle Ages record-keeping was more intensive: that there is simply more information about everything in the fourteenth century than in the ninth century. The fact that secularization and individualism in art grew (as far as evidence is concerned) in the later Middle Ages, shows up in Holt's list, with artists beginning to write about their own work from the mid-thirteenth century onwards whereas earlier there were only clerics recounting great building projects or travelogues. In the later Middle Ages too, we get more information about small commissions rather than just information about very large, important endeavours.

128   The fact that more laymen were artists and patrons in fifteenth-century Italy than in twelfth-century France did not mean that artistic products were much less religious in subject-matter or aim. Religion simply was not compartmentalized socially. It was perfectly acceptable that Benvenuto Cellini, the goldsmith, would don the habit if he managed to get a particularly lucrative papal office in the early sixteenth century, and conversely, for Bishops in the Ottonian Empire in the eleventh century to be fighting-men with castles and armies. 'Secularization' meant *only* that patrons and artists were less often clerics, and this trend had begun anyway when, in the later Middle Ages, more stabilized city and court life had developed away from the monastic monopoly forced on art during the invasion period of the earlier Middle Ages. In fifteenth-century Florence commissions by laymen, even for public squares and private houses, were dominantly religious or had very strong religious overtones.

129   As for individualism, when printing came in, one of the greatest fifteenth-century bibliophiles Federigo da Montefeltro of Urbino refused to have anything but individually written manuscripts in his collection. And it was not

until the sixteenth century that engraving provided a way of sending reproductions of great masterpieces all over Europe. Until then, amateurs of art had to live with the fact that an individual work could only be seen in one place. People did not possess our attitude to 'copying' anyway. They admired expert fakes because there were no machines to make reproduction seem facile. Artists spent their lives making 'Annunciations', 'Madonnas' and so on, and when the purpose of art is to teach religious truths and provide recognizable and movable devotional images, the function of communication is so strong that an 'Annunciation' or whatever must have many features in common with others of its type simply in order to be recognizable to worshipper and patron. In this situation, the artist's individualism lies in his subtlety of interpretation of well-known themes and the situation is the same in fifteenth-century Italy as it had been for a thousand years: he does not express paramountly his own feelings and thoughts and he does not have to decide what subject to represent.

130　We have also got to stress that there were plenty of non-secular, non-individualist facets in Renaissance art. I can think of four important fifteenth-century Italian artists who were also friars: Fra Giocondo, Fra Filippo Lippi, Fra Angelico and Fra Bartolomeo. Obviously papal patronage (as the careers of Raphael and Michelangelo show) was still of great importance. As to individualism – the reason why Ghiberti and Raphael were so successful was that they were experts at getting their numerous assistants to produce large schemes in a fine corporate style. Such corporate styles are also to be found in the great mediaeval monastic schools of illumination or in the building of great mediaeval cathedrals. The corporate habit is, after all, merely an efficient solution to the problem of creating a harmonious effect in a large project taking many years to complete. It wasn't until very recently that the isolated examples of Michelangelo painting the Sistine ceiling alone, or Leonardo late in life labouring single-handed on panels, became the artistic rule: that when an artist signed a work it really began to mean he had done it all himself. Taking an analogy, the mediaeval and Renaissance 'author' of an artistic work is more like our concept of the architect-designer: the 'ideas' man. Once you've accepted this concept of individuality it is not a great step to understanding the position where the *patron* (who feels *he* is the 'ideas' man and the 'director' of operations) signs a work – as you'll find Abbot Suger doing at St Denis in the twelfth century. Finally, the new phenomenon of artists writing about their work, and amateurs writing about them, doesn't mean that we know anything about their intimate thoughts and feelings. Except for the odd letter that has survived, we have to wait until the seventeenth century or even later for that sort of individualism. What we have are their ideas about art, and what is really significant about their writing about their work is that they begin to make a claim for the intellectual (not purely craft) status of art and artists. Their fight is paradoxically almost the opposite of emphasizing the emotional, personal character of art; to do with proving that art is a *theoretical* matter, worthy of scholarly attention, not something 'manual' like carpentry: that it requires individual attention, not to be mentioned merely in passing in books on other topics as in earlier times.

(ii) Artists and others on art: personnel; the purpose of art; naturalism

131　Please read the following passages: Theophilus (pp. 1–8); Villard de Honnecourt (pp. 88–91); Matthias Roriczer (pp. 95–101); and Cennini (pp. 136–50). Answer the following questions to focus your reading.

1   Why might one group Cennini and Theophilus separately from Honnecourt and Roriczer?

2   What sort of person do Cennini and Theophilus think the artist should be?

3   What does Theophilus think the purpose of art is?

4   Is mediaeval art naturalistic? What do Cennini, Honnecourt and Theophilus mean when they talk of 'drawing from life' and being 'beautiful and natural'? (Look carefully at Figures 12, 15, 25, 48 and try to apply what the three writers had to say about art, to them.)

132   1   Roriczer and de Honnecourt provide 'recipe books' for artists. Cennini and Theophilus include in *their* manuals some theory of what art is and should do, although it is interesting that it is not until late in the Middle Ages that a layman like Cennini takes this more intellectual approach, although even then he does not lay down the religious purposes of art in the way that Theophilus the monk does.

133   2   However both Cennini and Theophilus agree that the artist should be a pious man, though Cennini lays rather less stress on the humility of the artist in accepting that all his talent comes from God.

134   3   Cennini would accept Theophilus' definition of the purpose of art – as would most fifteenth-century Florentines. The ideas used by Theophilus are repetitions of the maxims of Pope Gregory the Great in the seventh century, which remained for nearly a thousand years the accepted view of the function of art. What does Theophilus say? Well, he quotes Old Testament precedents for God's approval of the way David and Moses embellished religion with visual images. Then he defines a threefold purpose for art: it impresses men with awe at the grandeur of creation by decorating churches splendidly; it relates the stories of the Bible in a way that teaches the truth and moves the spectator to devotion: ultimately it makes men turn to God; finally, it produces beautiful *utensils* for church ritual. And I must emphasize again (as I shall explain more fully in Unit 11) that this view of the function of art was still true for fifteenth-century Italy, and that even then it was not thought the business of the artist to redefine these aims. The manuals and treatises of this period are more elaborate than Cennini's, but they still do not trespass on clerical preserves.

135   4   What does Theophilus mean when he talks in his first paragraph of the 'beautiful and natural'? What did he think art's relationship to nature was? One rather negative way of looking at this is to say that mediaeval writers used Latin, had no particular tradition of art criticism of their own and tended to use concepts and artistic compliments that could be found in Latin writers like Pliny and Quintilian. So sometimes they use the term 'natural' very rhetorically and conveniently and certainly not with the sense that a classical writer would have applied to a classical sculpture. I think Leo of Ostia does this (p. 13 Holt) when he says that 'One would believe that the figures in the mosaics were alive and that in the middle of the pavement flowers of every colour bloomed in wonderful variety.' Renaissance art critics use this sort of compliment too: like standard inserted 'purple passages'.

136   There is a different way to look at this. You can say with Alois Riegl that all artists think (and are perfectly justified in doing so) that their images are 'natural' in some way. What Riegl meant was that all visual images are conventional systems of representation and that the human brain is so good at recognizing representations (even chance ones, let alone intended ones)

especially of the human figure, that there is absolutely no need for photographic 'verisimilitude'. A mediaeval artist or spectator had not seen a Van Eyck or a Praxiteles and might not anyway have thought them very realistic because he had not learnt their particular set of realistic conventions. So he could say with conviction '*that* is a landscape', 'this is a saint, a lion' or whatever, when presented with the familiar conventional image.

137   There is a third way of looking at this use of 'natural'; one which brings it very close to the term 'beautiful' and very far from the meaning 'so natural that it could be mistaken for the real thing': mediaeval and Renaissance writers, too, often use the term in the sense 'creative nature' rather than 'created nature' (*natura naturans* rather than *natura naturata*). They say 'this painting is as beautifully final and perfect a statement as a natural object' not that 'it is such an accurate representation of a flower that you feel you could pick it'. I think you can imagine such a statement being made about the mosaic apse of San Clemente meaning that the design seems so final and so 'right' in expressing the idea of the embracing joy of the tree of life (life after death as well as life on earth) through the suffering of Christ (the cross and the thorn bush) that you could not imagine another better solution: just as a product of nature – a celandine let's say – simply *is*, and a primrose is not a *better* solution, and indeed does not come into your liking for the celandine. God created all things in Nature and made them beautiful and harmoniously structured. He made man too, and infused in him some of His own creativity to make, now and then, with skill and ingenuity, objects which have something of the power, simplicity and 'rightness' of created Nature itself. Vasari had this in mind I think when he said that Giotto only had Nature as his teacher – not that Giotto suddenly went off and drew from life, so much as that he was able to make a creative break from the past in the way that Nature sometimes can, and that his work had the beauty of Nature. This is the sense behind the Renaissance use of 'natural and graceful' together as artistic compliments: the artist is praised for being 'natural' in the way Nature is in showing no sign of straining or contrivance. His work is 'easy'. I shall return to the definition of realism in Unit 10 and 13, but I hope I have shown that it is no good saying that, simply, mediaeval art is not naturalistic while Early Renaissance art is.

138   There is yet another consideration to take into account, though, in understanding both the mediaeval and Renaissance attitude to the 'real'. For one thing, if it is your business to create awesomely beautiful decorations in a church, to recreate events in the Bible and history of the Church which neither you nor your spectator have ever seen and which anyway have the most 'other worldly' significance, to explain Christian dogma (the Trinity for instance) and make ritual utensils, realism is not of very much use to you. You will want to use what you observe in the visual world as a sort of creative fuel – to give you ideas for decorative motifs on utensils or buildings. You will want to have familiarized yourself with useful forms in the visual world so that you can translate them into your notebook and use them in your various compositions. This is what Honnecourt is doing in his drawing of a lion 'from life'. You will need to observe *enough* to stock your mind with information enabling you to create figures, or whatever, on your panel which remind your spectator *sufficiently* to bring recognition. You will learn various useful tricks (Cennini's rocks which can be made into towering crags on your panel) to make effective representational shortcuts. Early Renaissance artists worked and were trained in this way too: their highest aim being to have drawn from life enough in their training to be able to draw any scene in their maturity *at will*. What characterizes Early Renaissance art is that the representational tricks are different (perspective, anatomy, proportion) and that as well as the formula there *is* an intensive rethinking, a reopening of the dialogue between the object

and the artist. But it remains true that Cennini-type crags can be found in late fifteenth-century images: Bellinis, Mantegnas, Leonardo's *Virgin of the Rocks* (Unit 13, Plate 3). It remains true, too, that once an artist's intensive training period was over he tended to rely on his or his school's formulae; only the formulae were new ones. And this was considered a virtue: being too realistic would bind the creative imagination and tie the representation so closely to an often ugly reality that the result would not be beautiful or symbolic enough. This is true of both mediaeval and Early Renaissance art. The attitude remains the same. The products look different because the formulae have been changed. The key thing is that the attitude of a mediaeval or Renaissance artist to what is real is very different from our own. For him, God is real and so are miracles. The rose is not just a beautiful flower, but in its blossoms and thorns an image created by God of the joy of salvation through the suffering of the martyrs. In the reality beyond commonsense dimensions, exist heaven and hell, the spiritual reality beyond the death and life of the body. The anagogical state of mind is part and parcel of this world-view as I shall explain in Unit 11. When an artist makes an image of a saint in a mediaeval illumination it is not a portrait of an individual (the artist probably would not know what the saint looked like anyway): he is making a devotional reminder. The saint needs no weight, mass, bodily volume, no specific lighting, landscape to move in, no transient characterful emotion and feeling or personal character. The very quality of sainthood was in his rejection of bodily stress and 'reality'. His significance *is* other-worldly. Given that fifteenth-century Florentines still shared this sort of world-view, why did they adopt visual formulae which did express weight and volume, mass and specific lighting, personal emotions, transient movement in representations? I shall try to explain this more fully in Unit 10 and 13. The key thing, I think, is that their audience wanted a more *dramatic* and *intimate* sense of other-worldly events. By giving holy figures some of the attributes of the real world they could *make* miracles, *create* the Crucifixion in the mind's eye and in the panel. And because their aim is *still* to represent a transcendental 'reality', they can use naturalistic formulae to make figures miraculous in the sense that they are more beautiful than commonsense reality. Further, they possess the Neo-Platonic idea that through loving beauty on earth the mind can aspire to more intellectual concepts of heavenly beauty. A naturalistically beautiful image, then, is a ladder to the transcendental concept of beauty. You will find Suger in the twelfth century using a variation of this idea (though not a naturalistic variation) in saying that, contemplating preciously jewelled decoration, he was led to meditate on the superlative preciousness of Heaven (Holt p. 30). In other words, the fact that Early Renaissance art looks different from mediaeval products does not mean that their artistic aims are any the less transcendental.

139   Skim through the accounts of Rome, Constantinople and the Holy Land (pp. 62–88). Read carefully the following passages: Leo of Ostia, Raul Glaber, St Bernard of Clairvaux, Abbot Suger, Abbot Haimon and Archbishop Hugo, Gervase of Canterbury (consecutively pp. 8–62) and the account of the building of Milan Cathedral (pp. 107–114). Please make notes answering the following questions.

1   Were artists and patrons in the Middle Ages very conservative and traditional in outlook?

2   What foreign or ancient art interested them?

3   Who were the major patrons, who actually built the churches and paid for the work?

4   What adjectives would you use to describe the general finished effect of

St Denis and Monte Cassino: is there a contrast between what is described and the way you usually think of mediaeval art?

(iii)   Innovation and tradition

140   Pro-Renaissance historians beginning with Vasari spread the idea that mediaeval patrons and artists were highly conservative. Now it is certainly true that *Italian* art in the Middle Ages clung very closely to Late Antique models and working methods but the patrons of Northern Europe were very adventurous, and even in the Italian, Desiderius, we get a vivid impression of a pioneer shouting down the caution of his advisers and boldly tearing down the old fabric of the basilica. A similar situation occurred in Rome when, in the early sixteenth century, it was decided to rebuild St Peter's. The sense of courage and conviction which covered Northern Europe with magnificent mediaeval churches is very apparent in Gervase of Canterbury and Suger and the report of Raul Glaber. You will find, that in spite of all their boasts, fifteenth-century Italian artists were not very conspicuous in their building endeavours: in transforming the landscape in a big way. Most of their energy was expended on adding to and decorating late-mediaeval buildings: adding sacristies, bronze doors, murals, tombs, façades, altarpieces and so forth. It is worth noting too, how stubborn Milanese craftsmen were in accepting the new ideas and expert advice of French and Flemish architects. Taking a very sweeping viewpoint too, I think we could well say that mediaeval art was as open as Renaissance art, if not more open, to a diversity of foreign styles: Byzantine and Arabic being the main ones. Fifteenth-century Italian artists tended to narrow their interest to the antique remains to be found on Italian soil in a rather more parochial way. Mediaeval artists were intermittently interested in classical art, but for the most part they were keen on incorporating large amounts of beautiful Roman masonry in their buildings or took over many classical forms unselfconsciously as part of tradition and did not *study* their structure devotedly in the Early Renaissance manner. What one must argue too is that since *both* mediaeval and Renaissance art have a religious function and need to communicate to a general congregation or audience, their work must have strong traditional links – in order to share enough of the spectator's visual language (made up of his visual *experience*) to be comprehensible. In other words, neither Donatello nor a thirteenth-century French illuminator can create such a new image of an Annunciation that it does not look like an Annunciation to *everyone*.

(iv)   Patronage

141   The three major buildings documented (Monte Cassino, St Denis and Canterbury Cathedral), were commissioned and built by monasteries. In the case of Monte Cassino, Byzantine craftsmen were imported, in the case of Canterbury, Frenchmen. At Monte Cassino and at St Denis faithful citizens assisted in the work. Desiderius was helped to get work done in Constantinople by the Emperor. Suger was helped by gifts from fellow clerics, kings, princes and noblemen. One wonders *quite* how willingly popular help was given in quarrying, particularly as all the sources mentioning this piety are clerics and there *is* a letter of Charlemagne's bemoaning the way monastic building preyed upon

the local people and exhausted the monks. Nevertheless we get a *picture* of clerical patronage and pious popular fervour, which is sometimes contrasted with the more business like and secular approach in the Early Renaissance, where committees of laymen or great noblemen are to be found along with clerical patrons getting work done largely by lay craftsmen. In fact, in Elizabeth Holt's selection of documents, the first lay patron of a huge building (the Duke of Milan and Milan Cathedral) appears late in the Middle Ages.

(v)   Media and effects

142   What did Monte Cassino and St Denis look like when they were completed? You may have thought that they looked very cluttered and gaudy. This is because, in Northern Europe, Reformation zealots battered sculpture and white-washed walls and because everywhere the delicate surface decorations of buildings have distintegrated. It is also because Early Renaissance artists and architects tended to value simplicity and asceticism in architecture, stopped painting sculpture, used murals rather than mosaic or stained glass and valued the 'skeletal' intellectual structure of drawing and shading rather than the use of colour. I think one could add, too, that we have been brought up to admire the (often promised but not executed) 'clean simplicity' of modern design, and that there simply *are not* many colourful buildings in our landscape.

143   For the mediaeval artist, painting sculpture made it more naturalistic, made it easier to discern shapes at a distance. Gold paint or gold mosaic backgrounds made the colours more sonorous; gold was useful for presenting jewellery on painted figures or haloes and was a splendid tribute to God's house. Stained-glass made very magical lighting effects inside a building. Putting jewels onto a book binding, a holy vessel, an altar sheltering relics, a statue, was a token of spiritual preciousness. Painting architecture emphasized the shapes of complex mouldings; (you can see the effect created in a manuscript illumination (Figure 25)). Oddly enough this mixing of media, use of precious material and gorgeous colour makes mediaeval art more 'classical' than that of the Renaissance. Most classical stone sculpture and buildings were painted. Statuary was given jewellery, metal locks of hair, ivory or painted eyes, metal armour or ornaments on drapery. Wooden figures were encased in ivory or precious metal plating. Walls were covered in brilliant mosaics and murals. Early Renaissance artists did not completely abandon 'mediaeval' media and effects. Ghiberti made stained-glass windows for the Cathedral of Florence. The della Robbia family put coloured glazes on terracotta sculpture. Verrocchio made a painted wooden Magdalen. Raphael used mosaic in the Vatican *stanze* and the Chigi chapel and some gold mosaic effects here too. But the trend was away from these media and effects. Alberti, in his treatise on painting in 1434, spurns the use of gold paint even when an artist has to imitate a golden object: better, he thinks, to show your skill in using yellow and white to feign the metal. The concept of a more ascetic art and architecture is partly based on the misguided idea that the pure, unadorned state of classical ruined buildings and sculptures was the original intended effect. It is also an admiration for the display of 'difficulty' and technical skill. It is more difficult to make a sculpted figure look 'alive' without the help of painted eyes and flesh tones. It is an emphasis on skill, and the sheer value of the *shape* of a building to reject costly embellishment and colour. But it is odd, that just that class of patron (the merchant-prince of Florence) whom you would expect to flaunt cost of materials, actually *prefers* virtuosity and simplicity. It is odd that fifteenth-century Florentines should be thought of as particularly interested in naturalism, and yet reject naturalistic colouring in sculpture.

144   I want, finally, to give a very *brief* survey of the media and techniques favoured by mediaeval artists and to try to contrast their selection with that of the Renaissance.

What does mediaeval painting consist of? What have survived most are illuminated manuscripts, often drawn in ink and coloured with tempera or water colours. Because they are so closely associated with the calligraphy and content of the text they are very illustrative (visual translations of words and concepts) and very decorative. Their audience would be rather elitist: those who could read or were allowed into monastic libraries. The popular painting was the mural. Very few of them have survived. Many of them imitate the effects of more precious mosaics. Just as, in a very strong sense, the illuminated book is a whole (each page harmonizing with its fellows), mosaics, murals and stained glass are all circumscribed in their form by the buildings they belong in, and are subordinated to this larger, decorative whole. Painting is either very big (murals, windows, mosaics) or very small (manuscripts). What there is very little of (except in late mediaeval Tuscany) is the medium-sized panel painted in tempera on wood and serving as an altarpiece or house decoration. Such panels, from the fifteenth century onwards, fill our art galleries and are very much a post-mediaeval phenomenon. The medium-sized panel (and after the fifteenth century the canvas) is a more independent form of painting than wall decoration or book illustration. It is not so much subordinated to (not attached so indelibly to) what it decorates. It is easier for it to become 'a work of art' just because it can become 'a gallery-object' – a collector's piece. The same sort of trend is apparent in sculpture. Most mediaeval sculpture is relief sculpture firmly attached to a building, a book, a religious utensil. There are a very few large, free-standing sculptures, though an increasing number of smaller ones from the thirteenth century onwards. There are not *that* many large Early Renaissance free-standing sculptures, but they are epoch-making ones, and also at this period there are some very small non-religious sculptures representing classical themes for a study or a palace.

These are the main contrasts in media, scale and location between mediaeval and Renaissance art. There is one other important area of contrast: that of technique. *Fresco* (painting with water soluble pigments on wet plaster) became very popular in the fifteenth and sixteenth century in Italy, whereas much mediaeval mural work had been executed in *secco* (painted onto a *dry* surface). There will be a television programme on this (TV 07). In sculpture, bronze was more highly valued (and more obtainable) than it had been before, and marble too – both media which had been valued by classical critics but which had often been replaced by wood and local stones in the previous centuries. I shall deal with this in detail in Unit 8.

145   I hope you will see that while there may be a lot of contrasts between mediaeval European art and Early Renaissance art in Tuscany, there are enough points of comparison to warrant extreme caution in neatly labelling styles as quite separate, and confidently naming a year or even a century where they 'began'. I hope, too, that this brief survey of mediaeval art will have persuaded you that mediaeval is not to be used as a foil to Renaissance art nor a mere hiatus between two similarly great styles, but one which forms a continuous link between the art of late antiquity, and that of the early fifteenth century.

Figure 1 Vault mosaic, S Costanza, *early fourth century, Rome (Alinari)*

Figure 2 Santa Sabina, *fourth century, Rome (Alinari)*

Figure 3   Santa Sabina,
exterior view (Alinari)

Figure 4   Doors
representing scenes from
the Old and New
Testaments, *wood, fourth
century, Santa Sabina,
Rome (Alinari)*

Figure 5   Christ with the writers of the Gospels represented symbolically, *wooden doors, Santa Sabina, Rome (Alinari)*

Figure 6   San Clemente, *rebuilt in the twelfth century using the ground plan of an early Christian basilica and sixth-century schola cantorum, Rome* (*Alinari*)

Figure 7   San Miniato al Monte, *interior, thirteenth-century marble choir and pulpit of church founded in 1060, Florence. Eleventh-century crypt beneath raised choir* (*Alinari*)

Figure 8 Mausoleum of Gall Placida, *Ravenna, fifth century* (*Alinari*)

Figure 9 S Maria Maggiore, *fourth century, Rome* (*early Christian mosaic apse remodelled by Jacopo Torriti, thirteenth century*) (*Alinari*)

Figure 10 S Cecilia in Trastevere, *twelfth-century façade using Late antique columns and twelfth-century tower with upper façade remodelled in the seventeenth-century,* Rome (*Alinari*)

Figure 11 Ambulatory of the Abbey of St Denis, *Paris 1140–4 (Foto Marburg)*

34

Figure 13 The Evangelist Matthew, Lindisfarne Gospels, *late seventh century, London, British Museum (Cotton Ms. Nero D.IV, fol. 25v) (British Library)*

Figure 12 Symbol of an Evangelist, Book of Durrow, *seventh century, Dublin, Trinity College Library (fol. 173v) (Board of Trinity College Dublin)*

Figure 14 Christ with Peter and Paul, S Prassede, S Pasquale, S Pudenziana and S Zenone, *apsidal mosaic, 817–24, S Prassede, Rome (Alinari)*

Figure 15   The Tree of Life, the Rood and the tree of thorns, *apsidal mosaic, c. 1200, San Clemente, Rome (Alinari)*

Figure 16   Monreale Cathedral, *decorated in mosaics between 1182 and 92, Sicily (Alinari)*

Figure 17 Adoration of Magi and Presentation at the Temple, *ivory book cover, Metz, late ninth or early tenth century* (*Victoria and Albert Museum, Crown copyright*)

Figure 18 Ascension of the Virgin, and bears giving food to St Gall, *ivory book cover, executed at St Gall by Tuotilo about 900* (*Cod. 53, Stiftsbibliothek, St Gallen*) (*Stiftsbibliothek St Gallen*)

Figure 19 Speyer Cathedral, *east end, early twelfth century* (*Mansell Collection*)

37

Figure 20   Durham
Cathedral, *1093–1133*
(*A. F. Kersting*)

Figure 21   Slaying of
Cain, *marble relief by*
'Wiligelmo', Modena,
1099–1106 (*Alinari*)

Figure 22   The Miracle
of St Clement, *eleventh-
century mural, lower church
of San Clemente, Rome*
(*Mansell Collection*)

Figure 23   Rheims
Cathedral, *west front,
1230s* (*spires never
completed*) (*Giraudon*)

39

Figure 25   Balaam and his ass, Psalter of St Louis,
*1252–70 (Bibliotheque Nationale, Paris, Ms. Lat. 10525
fol. 39v) (Bibliotheque Nationale)*

Figure 24   Virgin and child, *silver gilt, given by Jeanne
d'Evreux to Abbey of St Denis, 1339 (Giraudon)*

40

Figure 26   Cecilia in Trastevere, *interior showing ninth-century apsidal mosaic and marble ciborium signed by Arnolfo di Cambio, 1284* (Alinari)

Figure 27   Baptistry, *vault mosaic of Last Judgement with the Creation, Joseph and his brothers and life of St John the Baptist, 1270–1300* (Alinari)

Figure 28 Parish church of Corsignano (*later the town of Pienza*), *twelfth century* (*Alinari*)

Figure 29 Pisa Cathedral, *baptistry and campanile, eleventh – fourteenth centuries* (*Alinari*)

Figure 30   S Maria della Spina, *Pisa, begun 1330* (*Alinari*)

Figure 31   San Martino, Lucca Cathedral, *twelfth century* (*Alinari*)

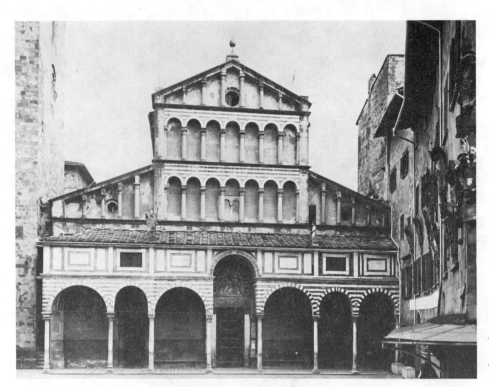

Figure 32   Pistoia
Cathedral, *fifth-century
foundation, rebuilt in the
twelfth century, with a
façade begun in 1311*
(*Alinari*)

Figure 33   San Michele,
*Lucca, begun twelfth
century with a mid-
thirteenth-century façade*
(*Alinari*)

Figure 34   San Miniato al Monte, *built in the eleventh century with a façade dating from 1070 to 1270 and a mosaic decoration of Christ with the Virgin and San Miniato dated 1260, Florence (Alinari)*

Figure 35   Baptistry, *sixth-century foundation, built 1059–1150(?) and roof completed 1128, Florence (Mansell Collection)*

Figure 36 Siena Cathedral, *west front, lower façade 1284–5, upper façade 1376, Siena (Alinari)*

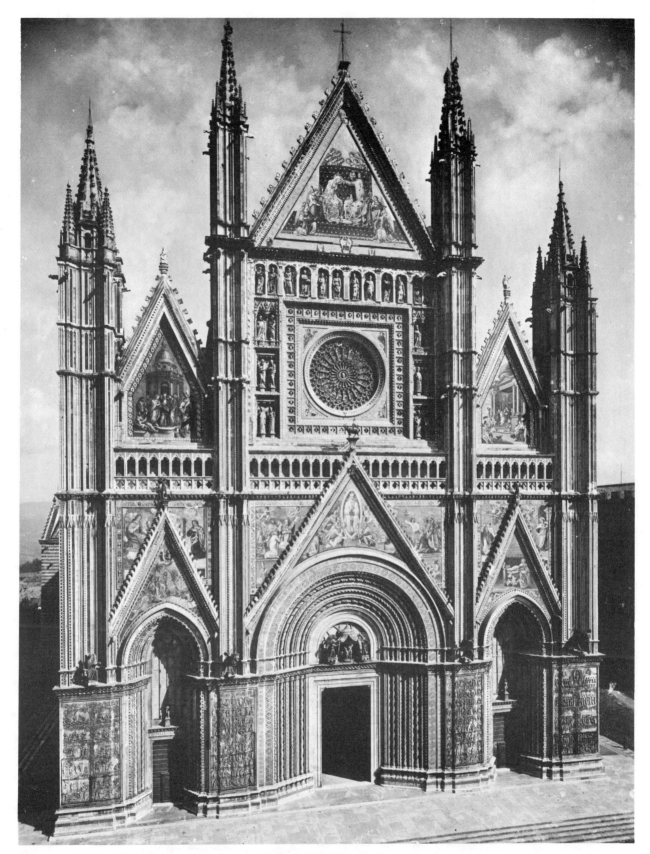

Figure 37   Orvieto Cathedral, *west front 1310 and after, Orvieto* (*Alinari*)

Figure 38 Laon
Cathedral, *1190–1200*
(*Jean Roubier*)

Figure 39 S Francesco,
*interior view facing altar
chapel, twelfth century,
Arezzo* (*Alinari*)

48

Figure 40   Pulpit, *marble,
Nicola Pisano, baptistry,
Pisa, 1259–66* (*Alinari*)

Figure 41   Adoration of kings (*detail cf. 40*) (*Alinari*)

Figure 42   Death of the Virgin, *exterior of south transept,
Strasbourg, c. 1230 (Foto Marburg)*

Figure 43 Bronze doors, *baptistry, Andrea Pisano, Florence, 1330–60 (Alinari)*

Figure 44 Madonna and Child, *marble, Tino da Camaino, Antonio Orso tomb, Bargello, Florence, 1321 (Alinari)*

Figure 45 The death of St Francis, *mural, Bardi Chapel, Giotto, Santa Croce, Florence (Alinari)*

50

Figure 46   Scrovegni Chapel, *murals, Giotto, c. 1300, Padua (Alinari)*

Figure 47   The Lamentation of Christ, *mural, Church of Panteleimon Nerez, Macedonia, 1164* (*Prestel Verlag, Munich*)

Figure 48   Presentation of the Virgin, *mural, Taddeo Gaddi, Santa Croce, Florence, 1338* (*Alinari*)

Figure 49 Presentation of Christ, *manuscript illumination, Les Très Riches Heures du duc de Berri, Pol de Limbourg, 1416 (Musée Condée, Chantilly) (Giraudon)*

Figure 50 St Louis altarpiece, *tempera on panel, Simone Martini, c. 1317 (Alinari)*

Figure 51   Altarpiece known as Maestà, *tempera on panel, rear face, Duccio, 1308–11, Museo del Opera del Duomo, Siena (Alinari)*

PART 2 EUROPEAN SOCIETY, ECONOMY AND POPULATION PATTERNS 1300–1600

by Margaret and Peter Spufford

CONTENTS

Introduction   57

The economic relationship between culture and society   58

The availability of money   60

The long thirteenth century of the commercial revolution   61
    Population growth to the early fourteenth century   61
    Increased cultivation   62
    Subdivision of peasant holdings   63
    Deterioration of peasant conditions and strength of landlords   63
    Extension of government and the birth of capital cities   65
    The commercial revolution of the long thirteenth century   66

Questions   68

The 'economic depression' of the Renaissance   68
    Population decline to the mid-fifteenth century   68
    Rising wages and falling prices   69
    Falling rents and abandoned land   70
    Fall in landed incomes and noble reactions   71
    Impotence of central government and shrinkage of towns   73

Questions   75

The long sixteenth century of the price revolution   76
    Population growth   76
    Rising prices, falling real wages and rising rents   76
    Rise in landed incomes, and incomes of gentry   76
    Renewal of government and taxation, and growth of capital cities   77
    The renewal of commerce   78

Questions   80

INTRODUCTION

200   The principal problem of the economic and social historian, as opposed to the political or constitutional or ecclesiastical or art historian, is that he is expected to make generalizations, rather than to write about individual men or institutions or works of theology or art. As William of Ockham (d. 1349) observed, only the individual has reality, the generality is only a name, something imposed by the mind. When we impose a generalization on a group of individual men or their actions, we are doing three things: not only abstracting and interpreting, but also making some sort of falsification, for the individual is all that is or was real. The farther we go from the individual the more false we are likely to be. We may make generalizations about the whole three hundred years from 1300 to 1600, but they can be refined by breaking down the period into a number of secular trends. The long thirteenth century of the 'commercial revolution' ended in the second quarter of the fourteenth century. The 'economic depressions of the Renaissance' lasted from the second quarter of the fourteenth century to the third quarter of the fifteenth. The long sixteenth century of the 'price revolution' ran from the third quarter of the fifteenth century to the second quarter of the seventeenth century. But even these generalizations are much too coarse, for within them every generation had a different feel. The generation that came to maturity after the plague of 1400 suffered less from the economic depression than either their parents around 1370, or their children around 1430. Population may have been rising from 1460 to 1620, but the effects of the population rise in the first generation of that rise, in an empty Europe of shrunken towns and deserted villages, were very different from those in the last generation at the end of the sixteenth century and the beginning of the seventeenth, when prices and rents were at their highest, real wages at their lowest, and the spectre of famine again stalked a Europe overfull of landless, unemployed vagabonds, in many ways much like that three hundred years before.

201   We may make generalizations about the whole of Europe, but they need to be refined in their applications to different countries as well as different generations. Germany was always far behind Italy in economic developments, and England still further behind. The 'commercial capitalism' which was already fully matured in Italy by the early fourteenth century did not reach Germany or England during that period of economic expansion. The techniques of the resident non-travelling merchants with their international many-branched firms, which had been evolved by Italian businessmen in that commercial revolution, were not adopted by south German businessmen until the fifteenth century at the beginning, or by English businessmen until the end, of the next period of expansion.

202   Even a whole country is too wide an area for generalization. Southern Italy and Sicily were different from Lombardy and Tuscany. Lombardy and Tuscany were different from each other, and the cities within Tuscany: Florence, Siena, Pisa, Lucca, Pistoi, all developed individually. In England the open fields of Oxfordshire were different from forest clearances of Warwickshire, or the ancient enclosed fields of Kent, or the sheep ranches of the Welsh marches. These different regional economies therefore supported different types of community. Even regional generalizations can prove false as soon as we look at individual village communities. We can find vividly contrasting communities even within the bounds of one small county, such as Cambridgeshire. However, in order that the human mind can grasp what was going on, we have to make generalizations, interpretative patterns out of the individual

realities, but we must always bear in mind that our generalizations are only our own inventions and in some degree falsifications, and it always helps to prevent our generalizations getting too far away from reality if we try to illustrate the points we are trying to make with something individual and real.

THE ECONOMIC RELATIONSHIP BETWEEN CULTURE AND SOCIETY

203   The music, painting, architecture and literature of the Renaissance was the production of a very limited part of society. Only the courts of Europe, and the major commercial cities, produced or patronized art and letters. Ghiberti, the sculptor, wrote 'I did not have to obey money, but gave myself to the study of art'. He listed the patrons who made this possible for him: the Malatesta ruler of the state of Pesaro and Rimini; the guild of importers and finishers of foreign cloth in Florence, who commissioned the bronze doors of the Baptistry of Florence; the commune of Siena; the order of Dominican friars, who commissioned a tomb for their general; Popes Martin V and Eugenius IV; and the guild of cloth manufacturers of Florence who financed the rebuilding of the Cathedral. (Look at the patrons in his account of his work in Elizabeth Holt (1947) *A Documentary History of Art*, pp. 156–63.) The Florentine bookseller, Vespasiano da Bisticci complained in the 1490s of the decline in letters when rulers' incomes or interests were diverted to other purposes:

204   We may see how numerous men of learning were in the times of Pope Nicolas of happy memory (Pope 1447–55), and of King Alfonso (King of Aragon and Sicily 1416, and of Naples 1443, d. 1458), because they were well-rewarded and held in the highest esteem, and how many excellent works they composed or copied through the munificence of princes so liberal as the two I have named, whose fame will last for ever. Moreover, beyond the money they gave, they paid high honour to men of letters and advanced them to high station. In addition to these two princes must be named a worthy successor, the Duke of Urbino (Federigo de Montefeltro, count of Urbino 1444, duke 1474, d. 1482), who having followed their example in honouring and rewarding and promoting men of letters, became their protector in every respect, so that all were wont to fly to him in case of need. Thus to help him in their labours, he paid them well for their work, so that he gained immortal fame by their writings. But when there was no longer a Duke of Urbino, and when neither the court of Rome nor any of the other courts showed any favour for letters, they perished, and men withdrew to some other calling, seeing that, as I have said, letters no longer led to profit or reward. (From the introduction to his lives of illustrious men quoted in Elizabeth Holt, *op. cit.* p. 182.)

205   At first sight, therefore, the social history relevant to 'the Renaissance' should deal only with the history of the ruling, noble, and upper commercial families. But these families cannot be studied in isolation, because they drew their income from the rest of society. Change in this major part of society, which was composed of peasants who made up over ninety per cent of the population of Europe, was therefore reflected in the incomes and spending power of princes, courtiers, noblemen and international merchants. Through them and the patronage that they were able and willing to extend, the incomes of architects, sculptors, musicians, scholars and authors were affected.

206   The surplus of the labour of the peasant and the craftsman had to be transferred through the tax-man and the rent-collector to the prince and the nobleman. Only then could it be used to pay for luxury goods, if it was not diverted to political expenditure, of which war was by far the most expensive.

Marxism

207   Luxury goods were primarily the material extravagances brought by international merchants over vast distances to the courts and capitals of Europe. In 1328 a single Swedish noble customer bought the following supplies for his household from a German merchant:

   1½ lbs of saffron, which had come from Spain or Italy
   90 lbs of almonds, from the Mediterranean
   4½ lbs of ginger, from India
   ½ lb 'grains of paradise'[1], which had come across the Sahara from West Africa
   1 lb cinnamon, from Ceylon
   6 lbs pepper, from the Malabar coast of India
   3 lbs of aniseed, from South Germany
   3 lbs of 'galangal'[2], from South-east Asia
   105 lbs rice from Spain
   4 lbs sugar from Spain
   1 barrel of Rhine wine
   2 barrels of French wine

The rents of the peasants resident on this nobleman's estate in Scandinavia were thus paying for the movement of goods across the Sahara and the Indian Ocean.

(As you read the whole of this section, refer to the maps in Units 1 and 2, particularly that of 'towns and trade routes in the later middle ages'. Make yourself familiar with the whereabouts of all the places we mention. Remember that the towns and fairs marked on the 'towns and trade routes' map are made to look of equal size and importance, but they were not.)

208   Luxury goods could also of course be immaterial, from the establishment of a *scriptorium* for copying manuscripts, to the payment of musicians, or the foundation of a university. From the thirteenth century to the sixteenth, rulers, from the greatest like the Emperor Frederick II at Naples in 1224, downwards to the Landgraves of Thuringia at Leipzig in 1409, founded universities as a matter of prestige, and to provide themselves with graduates for their civil services.

209   Here is the foundation charter of the University of Naples:

   Frederick by the grace of God Emperor. . . . We order that at Naples, loveliest of all cities, all the professional arts shall be taught and a seat of studies shall be established so that all those hungry for knowledge will find in my kingdom the wherewithal to satisfy their needs and will not be compelled to seek our foreign nations for the sake of studies. In doing so we intend to promote the welfare of our republic and at the same time, through our special generosity and affection, we wish to provide for the needs of our subjects. . .
   We invite all studious men to serve us; those who persevere in their studies will earn praise and reward since we will entrust them with the administration of law and justice. . .

Thomas Aquinas was one of the first undergraduates to take the arts course there. The careers of men like St Thomas, free to spend their whole lives in philosophical and theological speculation and teaching, were the greatest luxury of all.

The revenues of the ruling house of Champagne were derived in the twelfth and thirteenth century partly from the land, already famous for grain, wine and wool, and partly from tolls on the great international trade fairs of Champagne, where the merchants of Italy met those of Paris and Flanders. The volume of business done at these fairs was rising rapidly in the late twelfth century when the court of Champagne at Troyes was becoming most notable

[1] 'Grains of paradise': capsules of a West African plant used as a spice and drug.
[2] 'Galangal': probably 'galingale', an aromatic East Indian root used in cookery and medicine; mildly ginger.

for its literary patronage, and Marie, dowager countess and regent of Champagne, was supporting both Andreas Capellanus and Chretien de Troyes amongst others. Here 'state' taxes, and tolls on international trade and the peasants of the ruler's own estates, were together paying for the development of Romance and the Courts of Love. In the same way the rents, surplus produce and taxes paid by the peasantry of the Malatesta state, the papal states, the duchy of Urbino and the kingdom of Naples, together with the profits taken from the labour of their employees by the masters of the guilds of cloth finishers and manufacturers of Florence, were ultimately paying for the humanism of Vespasiano and his authors and the sculpture of Ghiberti.

210 So the social historian interested in the Renaissance must first consider the apparently irrelevant peasantry of Europe, and the changes in their expendable surplus caused by over and under-population. Population changes determined the changing incomes of the whole of society, and so, on this peasantry the whole superstructure of society rested, from at least the twelfth century through the period of the Renaissance and Reformation to the Industrial Revolution.

THE AVAILABILITY OF MONEY

211 A number of steps were necessary to transform the labour of peasants on the land into oriental spices or humanist rhetoric, or 'renaissance' buildings. At each of these steps a developed marketing system and an adequate supply of money were required. So, before we consider the condition of the peasantry in western Europe and the way the population of Europe rose and fell between 1300 and 1600, it is necessary to get rid of the popular misconception that in the Middle Ages European society did not use money as a medium of exchange, but depended exclusively on barter.

212 Money, which had circulated throughout the Roman Empire, went on circulating, as in antiquity, throughout the Middle Ages, except temporarily in England, where it fell out of use from the fifth to the seventh centuries. In the tenth century the use of coinage was extended across the Rhine to 'Saxony' and Bavaria, and further to Denmark and Bohemia, in the eleventh century to Hungary, and in the twelfth century to Poland, Sweden and Scotland. However, until the twelfth century the ordinary peasant tenant farmer handled no more than a few silver pennies each year, for which he sold a small part of his produce, and with which he paid a small part of his rent. In the twelfth century this changed. New sources of silver were discovered in the Erzgebirge (Ore mountains) and the eastern Alps, at Freiberg and Friesach. When these silver mines were exhausted, a succession of new discoveries were made, replacing each other in turn, that were not finally exhausted until the mid-fourteenth century. As a consequence, silver was more plentiful in Europe in the early fourteenth century than at any time before the early seventeenth century, or possibly even the early nineteenth century. Even the silver bullion families of the late fourteenth and mid-fifteenth centuries did not lead to a complete breakdown in the use of money, although they did act as a serious brake on the economy. From the 1460s new sources of silver became available, both in the Erzgebirge and the Alps, at the Scheeberg in Saxony and at Schwaz in the Tirol, which, with their successors, lasted to the mid-sixteenth century, when the silver mines of Zacatecas in Mexico and Potosi in Peru took over.

213 By 1300 a highly developed system of markets and fairs had come into existence throughout Europe so that peasants could easily obtain money for their

surpluses of grain, wine, wool, oil or cattle. Even if it was disrupted from time to time in the later fourteenth and early fifteenth centuries this marketing system never completely broke down. It was revised and expanded in the sixteenth century, so that throughout the period from 1300 to 1600 it was generally possible for a peasant to find a purchaser for his produce.

214   Since people's dependence on food was much more evident then than it is in our own society, the struggle for bread, or gruel, must occupy a very high place in our discussion of the economic and social structure. The relationship between the number of men and the amount of land on which they had to live was vital, not only to villagers, but also to landlords, and, at a not very distant remove, to townsmen also.

215   What proportion of the money obtained by the peasant for his produce could be extracted from them by their landlords and their rulers may have depended in the short run on law and force, but it depended in the longer run on supply and demand; on the supply of land and the demand for it; on this vital relationship between men and land. The supply of land in Europe was relatively inelastic, but the demand for it and its products altered enormously between the twelfth century and the sixteenth. When population was rising and high, up to the early fourteenth century, land was hard to find and landlords could impose what conditions they liked on their tenants. When population was falling and low, as it was later in the fourteenth century and in much of the fifteenth, tenants could pick and choose, and landlords had to be content with what they could get. When the population increased again, as it did from the end of the fifteenth century right on until the next decline in the seventeenth century, conditions improved again for the landlords and deteriorated for their peasant tenants.

THE LONG THIRTEENTH CENTURY OF THE COMMERCIAL REVOLUTION

Population growth until the early fourteenth century

216   In 1300, most parts of Europe had reached or were nearing the end of a long period of population growth. In a few places the highest population point had already been passed, as in parts of rural Tuscany around Pistoia (see Herlihy in A. Molho (1969) *Social and Economic Foundations of the Italian Renaissance*, pp. 77–90). This high point, when it was reached, was the maximum that the land could sustain, given the then relatively primitive state of agricultural technology. We do not have enough evidence to be precise about the population of wide areas of Europe. Much of Italy is too mountainous to bear more than a sparse population, but Lombardy and Tuscany were perhaps the most densely populated parts of all Europe. Various historians have estimated that the whole peninsula had some nine or ten million inhabitants. France, a bigger country, had the largest overall population, and at its early fourteenth-century maximum had some nineteen to twenty-one million inhabitants. England was only slightly less thickly populated and had between four and a half and six million people. Germany was more thinly peopled, with only eleven and a half to fourteen million people. Altogether, some fifty-five to sixty million people lived in western Europe, with a sparse thirteen to fifteen million people in eastern Europe. That may not seem many, but historians estimate that the population

was almost double what it had been a century and a half earlier. Moreover, the total populations estimated for France and England were not to be reached again until the eighteenth century. In many areas of northern France and in some parts of England the same level of population was not reached again until the nineteenth century, if ever. It was only the 'agricultural revolution', the widespread eighteenth-century adoption of new agricultural techniques 'invented' in the seventeenth century, that allowed Europe to pass this early fourteenth-century population level. At the end of the eighteenth century there were many, like Malthus, who were afraid that doom lay round the corner.

217 Malthus' prophecies may not have been fulfilled in the nineteenth century, but they were amply fulfilled in the fourteenth. People in western Europe were so numerous that a bad harvest meant famine, and two consecutive bad harvests meant widespread death from starvation. In 1315–17, two bad harvests afflicted all Europe north of the Alps and the Pyrénées. An enormous death toll resulted. In the heart of industrial Flanders, ten per cent of the population of the textile town of Ypres perished in a few months. In the depths of rural England, enormous numbers of tenants died on the Bishop of Winchester's estates. A similar succession of two bad harvests hit all southern Europe twenty-five years later and once again men died of starvation. Even what Dr Larner in Unit 5 calls the 'mature economy' of early fourteenth-century Florence was not immune to harvest failure and its fatal consequences. Perhaps as many as fifteen thousand Florentines perished, out of ninety thousand, at a time when their city was the banking centre of Europe. And these were only the two worst pairs of years in the first half of the fourteenth century.

Increased cultivation

218 The enormous increases of population through the twelfth and thirteenth centuries which had built up to this state of drastic over-population in the early fourteenth century had brought about a radical change in the vital relationship between men and land. Attempts had been made throughout Europe to increase the amount of land under cultivation. Newly cleared forest land or newly drained fen tended to prove fertile. But inhospitable mountainsides or marginal heathland often did not. The search for more land took place at every level. On the largest scale whole new provinces were colonized east of the Elbe by people who migrated long distances from over-populated areas of Flanders, Holland, Zealand and West Germany to settle the vacant Baltic coastlands and the potentially fruitful grainlands of the north European plain behind them.

219 This colonization progress had begun around 1100, was at its most vigorous between 1120 and 1300, and did not come to an end until the middle of the fourteenth century. The migrants who came to the 'frontier' of Europe were organized by recruiting agents who looked for potential frontiersmen in over-populated areas, offering them tenancies of ample farms at low cash rents, with ten or even twenty years guaranteed freedom from taxation as an additional incentive. The settlement of Brandenberg and Pomerania was advertised in the words 'The country is excellent, rich in meat, honey, poultry, and flour; therefore come hither, you Saxons and Franconians, men from Lorraine and from Flanders, for both can be obtained here: deeds for the salvation of your souls and settlement on best land'.

220   On a much smaller scale new settlements were being made all over Europe. Enterprising lords were transforming forest to more profitable agricultural land, recruiting tenants to clear and settle on favourable terms, whether in eastern France or in the wooded areas of Warwickshire or Staffordshire. In south-western France, Alfonse of Poitiers, as Count of Toulouse, and his neighbour, Edward of England, as Duke of Aquitaine, were among those creating *bastides*, new villages and new towns by the hundred to fill out the gaps in previously settled areas. And at the lowest level, assarts or breaches were made by the villagers themselves in the common land and waste land around the individual village settlements. The rural lordships around Nîmes in Languedoc had a population increase of twenty-three per cent in one generation between the hearth lists of 1293 and those of 1322. This increase mainly took place on the desolate garrigues, a blasted heathland, which today scarcely supports goats. The hard-pressed inhabitants of the countryside around Pistoia in Tuscany farmed ever further up the mountainsides of the Appenines. Much of this new land produced the most meagre of crops and had soon to be abandoned. If it remained in cultivation it reduced the amount of grazing for village livestock and so reduced the amount of natural fertilizer for the whole village and therefore reduced yields. This sort of over-extension of agriculture, combined with a certain climatic deterioration in the early fourteenth century made for the succession of harvest failures. Languedoc was desolated by dearth twenty years out of forty-six between 1302 and 1348.

Subdivision of peasant holdings

221   Besides those who set off for newly ploughed land, more and more men were crammed into existing settlements. Peasant farms were broken down by inheritance into minute parcels. At Rozoy, in the Paris basin, a quite substantial peasant farm of 160 arpents (an arpent was a little less than an acre) became divided by inheritance processes into 78 plots. It is now realized that a fifteen-acre holding of arable land was the minimum which could support a peasant family. In East Anglia, the Hundred rolls as analysed by Kosminsky showed that in the 1270s as many as forty-six per cent of the peasants had too little land to support themselves on and had to supplement their farming by working for wages, either on the lord's demesne, or on the farms of the small minority (three and a half per cent) of peasants who held farms larger than the traditional thirty acres and were employers of labour. The situation in densely populated Flanders was even worse. Analysis of holdings on an estate of the count of Flanders near Ghent has shown that by the mid-fourteenth century four out of every five tenants held plots too small to subsist on. But it was possible to eke out a livelihood by earning wages in nearby Ghent, the most important woollen cloth manufacturing city of northern Europe.

Deterioration of peasant conditions and the strength of landlords

222   This super-abundance of rural population left peasants completely at the mercy of their lords, many of whom took advantage of the situation, so that seigneurial burdens were often at their heaviest in the early fourteenth century. This does not mean that labour services were at their heaviest then. Most landlords in western Europe had decided much earlier that they preferred money-rent to labour-rent or rent in kind. Such a change when it was first made was to the

lord's advantage and very much against that of the tenant. The lord gave the tenant back his labour and asked him for money instead. This compelled the tenant to work his own land more intensively, and to tighten his belt very considerably to create a surplus which he could sell on the market and so pay his rent as well as feed his family. In the long run it might well work to the advantage of the tenant, since the thirteenth-century price rise eroded the burden of a cash rent, unless the lord could put it up. The earliest moves away from labour-rent to money-rent took place in Italy, where they began on a considerable scale in the eleventh century. In France there was, in Bloch's words a 'prodigious attenuation of agricultural services' in the twelfth century. In Bavaria, the twelfth century also marked the beginning of the end for labour services. On the newly settled eastern frontier of Germany there never had been labour services. The tenants had all been free men from the time of settlement and only paid cash rents. On the Spanish frontier of Europe, reconquered bit by bit from the Moors, similarly free frontiersmen peasants, arms-bearing and horse-riding *caballeros villanos*, were to be found, alongside big estates worked by wage labour. Only in England did labour services survive to any extent until the late thirteenth century. Even there, in the area picked out by Kosminsky as having the heaviest burden of labour services, sixty-one per cent of the rent was money-rent and only thirty-nine per cent was labour-rent. But then English landlords, like some West German landlords, often continued to keep demesne farms, which they even augmented by buying out, or otherwise easing out their own tenants. They manned these demesne farms with wage labour and sold their products on the market. Their French or Italian counterparts on the other hand had long before given up agriculture themselves and leased out the demesne in blocs to tenants.

223   Whether they took the rents from their increasing numbers of tenants in cash, or in kind, or even still in labour services in backward areas like England, landlords by the early fourteenth century were usually profiting enormously from the state of over-population. Cultivation of crops for the market had become the normal thing to do, whether it was undertaken by the peasants to meet their lords' exactions, or by the lords themselves.

224   How then did landlords increase the burdens on their tenants? By straight-forwardly increasing the cash rent if custom permitted. In Italy, landlords sought first to reduce perpetual hereditary tenancies to leases for single lives when opportunity, such as escheat for lack of heirs, permitted, and then to transform these into leases for shorter and shorter terms of years. On each occasion the cash rent could be increased. In England the perpetual hereditary tenancy was still the custom by the early fourteenth century, but the landlord could demand an entry-fine from the incoming tenant when a son succeeded his father. There was nothing to prevent these from being very large, and if the son could not or would not find the money, it was easy enough to incorporate the land in the demesne or find someone who was prepared to sink himself into debt to have some land to farm. The lord could also exploit his monopolies of brewing and milling and baking, by charging excessive fees, and by preventing evasion of the monopoly, by breaking hand-querns for example. He could also exploit the fees due on death and on marriage, and make a quite considerable income out of his tenantry from the fees and fines due from the manorial court. Finally he could exploit the grievance caused by all this exploitation, by offering to sell freedom from it for a round lump sum. On royal estates in France, Louis IX (1224–74) began selling such freedom to whole villages, and Louis X (1314–16) went to the stage of compelling all the remaining villeins on royal estates to buy their freedom.

225   Rural lords were not the only members of society to profit from forced freedom. In 1256–7 the commune of Bologna gave 6000 *servi* in the surrounding countryside the right 'to resume the perfect and perpetual liberty' granted to man in paradise. The *servi*, having become free men, were now liable to communal taxation, and the same act that gave them their liberty compelled them to register for taxation in a register ironically known as the *Paradisus*.

226   Most acts of manumission were for a cash benefit of this kind to the lord, and might even be resented by those forcibly freed, when they were mulcted of yet more money in the process. Modern historical study tends to emphasize the economic rather than the legal situation of the peasantry. People do not have to be 'unfree' to be oppressed. They are oppressed if they are starving, overpopulated, and lack bargaining power. But legal unfreedom (i.e. serfdom) when it survived became felt as oppression in the fourteenth century when the peasantry's economic position had improved and they had a new collective bargaining power, yet were baulked by obsolescent legal restrictions. In the over-populated thirteenth century, the vital issue had been survival, not freedom.

227   As a consequence of these changes the manorial system in most parts of Europe was dying, and in some places was already dead, when the fourteenth century opened. Any idyllic patriarchal relationship between lord and man, if, that is, it had ever existed, had been replaced by a callous cash nexus between landlord and tenant. The forms of manorialism survived, even in some places to the twentieth century, but the life had gone from the body.

228   You will notice that we have used 'manorial' to describe this system, and not 'feudal'. We have specifically not used 'feudal' as it is such an ambiguous term. 'Feudal' may describe any sort of dependent relationship; or slightly more narrowly, any kind of dependent relationship based on service, most often military or agricultural, depending on which social levels are under discussion. We range ourselves amongst those historians who, for convenience, limit the use of 'feudal' to the organization of the upper ranks of west European society between the ninth and thirteenth centuries in which particular jobs, keeping a county or a castle, fighting as a knight, were paid for with landed estates known as fiefs, or in latin *feuda*, from which the system was named. We distinguish this from the tenancy of farm land lower in the social scale, paid for by the peasant tenant with a complex of obligations, among which labour-rent often predominated. We describe the latter as the 'manorial' or 'seigneurial' system, and it is this that was dissolving into a more modern landlord and tenant relationship by the early fourteenth century.

Extension of government and the birth of capital cities

229   The receipt from the twelfth century onwards of rent in money rather than goods or services meant that landlords were no longer tied to their estates, and this fitted in with the gravitation of rulers to fixed points in their territories. Instead of moving around from estate to estate they too remained in one place for long periods. With their income being received in money, rulers were able to replace their primitive households of hereditary officials, paid by grants of land, with the beginnings of 'bureaucracies' of professional administrators paid with money wages. In this way capitals began to form around the points at which rulers settled, with their nascent permanent organs of government around them, and their greater subjects in attendance. In twelfth century France such capitals grew up at Poitiers, for the counts of Poitou who were

also dukes of Aquitaine; at Troyes for the counts of Champagne, and at Toulouse for the counts of Toulouse; as well as for the kings of France in Paris. These courts were the nurseries of European culture. Here young noblemen who had completed their education and were still waiting for their inheritances clustered until they could inherit and marry. In this milieu the rulers patronized writers of courtly literature, or wrote it themselves, from William IX of Aquitaine at Poitiers at the beginning of the twelfth century, through his grand-daughter Eleanor, in turn Queen of France and of England, to his great-grand-daughter Marie, Countess of Champagne, who patronized Andreas Capellanus and Chretien, at her court at her capital at Troyes.

230   As the wealth available to landlords, and particularly to princes, increased, courts became fewer and greater. By the end of the thirteenth century, several local capitals had been subsumed in one great capital, at Paris, the biggest city in Christendom. The King of France was by now also Count of Champagne, Count of Poitou and Count of Toulouse, and the former capitals at Troyes, Poitiers and Toulouse were empty of their former glory. The wealth of France was increasingly concentrated in one city. To Paris came the revenues of state.

231   In the thirteenth century rulers introduced a variety of national taxes on their subjects. National assemblies grew up to represent these subjects, 'or the weightier part thereof', and granted subsidies, land taxes, hearth taxes, sales taxes and customs dues. Seekers after royal justice also came to Paris, as well as provincial administrators referring to the central administration. Increasingly the greatest noblemen from all parts of France, and indeed lesser noblemen too, came to build for themselves permanent *hotels* (grand town-houses) in Paris, to live there for long periods and to spend there the revenues from their estates scattered throughout France. This enormously stimulated trade, particularly luxury trades, as well as artistic works, which were in some sense the luxury trades of the mind.

232   The kings of England built up a similar capital at Westminster, with the nobility living in inns along the Strand between Westminster and London, or in London itself. The rulers of Naples and Sicily did the same in Naples and Palermo. The popes did the same at Rome, and later at Avignon. In Germany, where there was no strong central authority, mini-capitals developed in the fourteenth century for the houses of Wittelsbach, Habsburg, and Luxemburg at Munich, Vienna, and Prague, but these cities were insignificant compared with the great capitals of western Europe. Rather more important were the capitals of the new princes of Lombardy, of the Visconti rulers at Milan and of the della Scala in Verona.

The commercial revolution of the long thirteenth century

233   These capitals, whether 'giant' cities of a hundred thousand inhabitants like Paris and Milan, or lesser ones like Munich and Verona, acted not only as potential centres of artistic patronage, but also as focal points for the demand for material luxury goods. They attracted enterprising merchants who supplied luxuries to court and courtiers, rulers and nobility. As the demand grew and trade expanded, a change in business methods took place which has been called a commercial revolution. Just as the industrial revolution was a revolution in industrial techniques, so this earlier commercial revolution was one in commercial techniques. The single merchant, who purchased his goods in one place, and went with them to sell them in another, gave way to the sedentary merchant who remained in his country house and entrusted his goods to

professional carriers. These conveyed the goods to his full-time agents (or factors) who were permanently resident abroad and with whom he kept in contact by regular correspondence. Once this crucial division of labour had taken place, it became possible to engage in complementary trades with several different places at once. So the many-branched firm came into existence with a head office in, let us say, Florence and permanent branch offices spread out from London to Famagusta, from Bruges to Rhodes.

234 The primitive peripatetic merchant took with him *in commenda* (commended to his care) investments in cash or goods from friends and relatives as well as his own goods, but such investments were for particular journeys only. The new business firms had complete shareholding patterns. Partnerships were made for periods of several years at a time to undertake a multiplicity of enterprises in a wide variety of places. The shareholders proper included not only the active directors of the company, but others who wished to invest in this way, and the capital was increased by further interest-bearing deposits placed in the business by the same people and also by others – who included many noblemen with liquid assets. Cardinals would invest through the branch at the Papal curia and English earls through the London branch. An excellent description of this revolutionary new style of business and all its concomitants, double-entry book-keeping, marine insurance and so forth is to be found in Hay (pp. 375-382).

235 Such new methods of trading began to be adopted first on the routes from Italy to the Levant where the whole luxury demand of the rulers and nobility of western Europe was concentrated, from Venice, Genoa and Pisa to Acre, Alexandria and Constantinople. They then spread within Italy in internal trade, and across the Alps to the fairs of Champagne. Eventually, by the end of the thirteenth century, the single agent who remained all the year in Champagne moving around from fair to fair, was replaced by permanent branches in the capital cities of Paris and London, and also in Bruges. The change only took place when concentrated demand developed. In fact, apart from Paris, London and Bruges, Italian companies did not find it worthwhile to plant branches outside the Mediterranean. Not even the trade of the Hanseatic merchants of the North Sea and the Baltic was big enough to warrant this division of labour in this period of expansion up to the fourteenth century. The great commercial cities which grew up at the nodal points of trade were, apart from Bruges, mostly to be found in Italy (see table in para. 266 for the very largest). The commercial towns of the less developed parts of Europe were much smaller. Early fourteenth century Lubeck, the largest port on the Baltic, was only about a tenth of the size of Genoa, and no English town except London was anything like as big as Lubeck.

236 The growth and focusing of luxury demand in capital cities led to the growth and focusing of commerce to supply that luxury demand in a limited number of commercial cities, and this in turn led to the growth of luxury industries to supply that commerce. The greatest industry of pre-industrial Europe, and indeed one of the leading sectors in industrialization, was the textile industry. Textile manufacture could sometimes be found in the same place as the trade in cloth, but sometimes in separate cities not far away. In the early fourteenth century, Florence was both a commercial city and an industrial city, with the same entrepreneurs engaged in arranging for the purchase of English wool, in managing the various textile manufacturing processes in and around Florence itself, and in organizing the sale of finished luxury cloth on the Naples market. At the same time, in Flanders, Bruges was the great commercial city, and the dependent textile industry was to be found in Ghent and Ypres nearby.

237 By the fourteenth century, a few cities – capitals, commercial cities, industrial

cities, or cities combining these functions – stood out from the general run of small towns, with a handful of craftsmen, weekly markets and annual fairs. These stretched across Europe from the Atlantic to the Pripet marshes, provided the local marketing system for the peasants of Europe and allowed them to specialize for the market in whatever they could grow best, whether wheat or wine, wool or oil. In these great cities with all their perils from disease and lack of sanitation, opportunity lay open to those who could take it. They acted as giant magnets for hopeful aspirants to fortune who continuously flowed into them by the thousand. The vast majority found only a premature grave, but a big enough minority of Dick Whittingtons made good to lend credence to the belief that the streets of London (or Milan, or Paris or Genoa) were paved with gold.

QUESTIONS

238   Answer the following questions to your own satisfaction. If you cannot do so, look back and check.

   1   Was Europe predominantly urban or rural in 1300? And in 1600?

   2   Why was the condition of the peasantry relevant to that of the rulers, the nobility, and the gentry?

   3   Was the money supply plentiful in 1300?

   4   Was labour-rent still common in Europe in 1300?

   5   By what standards was Europe densely populated in 1300?

   6   Name three ways in which new land was cleared in the thirteenth century.

   7   Why was the bargaining power of the peasantry low when the population was high?

   8   Why were rulers able to settle at fixed points in their realms from the twelfth century onwards?

   9   How did capitals stimulate luxury trade?

   10   What was the 'Commercial Revolution' of the thirteenth century?

THE 'ECONOMIC DEPRESSION' OF
THE RENAISSANCE

Population decline to the mid-fifteenth century

239   The population of Europe had reached or exceeded its limits well before the Black Death and in many places had even fallen somewhat before the first wave of plague struck. The first wave of plague is well described in Boccaccio, but the effect of wave after wave of plague needs to be brought home. Had there been only one wave of plague the effect would have been no more than that of an ultra-severe famine. The oldest surviving parish register in Europe, that of Givry in Burgundy, shows not only the enormous scale of deaths, but also the wave of weddings that succeeded those deaths: weddings of men and women who had suddenly inherited farms and were able to marry and set up house

unexpectedly. It then shows the natural baby-boom that followed. It took something like three waves of plague before the situation of over-population was really dented, and a variety of trends went into reverse.

Rising wages and falling prices

240   Agricultural prices had been moving steadily upwards through the thirteenth century as the increasing demand of more men for food was less and less met by the far more slowly increasing supply of food from more land. This reached ruinous heights in the starvation years of the first half of the fourteenth century. The immediate effect of the plagues was often to raise prices for a year or two as labour shortages in agriculture sorted themselves out, but in the long run there was a dropping of prices, and this really began after three waves had had their effect. Prices of grainstuffs went on dropping once they had started to go down, well into the fifteenth century. By this we mean the averaged prices over a number of years, for the prices in individual years moved up or down very violently according to the quality of the yield of that year's harvest. It is in some sense a piece of historian's falsification to pick out long-term trends in prices, since individual men bought and sold grain not at averaged prices, but at particular prices determined by the particular circumstances of that place in that year, and in that year only. Men only starved to death once, and averaging out the prices which had caused them to do so, softens the impact on us of the brutal physical facts. The economist Keynes once commented on this type of 'long range' thinking when he said pithily 'in the long run we are all dead'.

241   Wages reacted rather more rapidly than prices. Wages had been as depressed by over-population as prices had been increased. After only one wave of plague, wages moved rapidly upwards. The effect on wages was the more marked because the marginal surplus of wage labour was removed at one blow. Men who might have expected to spend the rest of their lives as wage labourers suddenly had the opportunity of becoming tenant farmers by inheritance of farms from dead relatives or by invitation of a landlord or his bailiff to step into dead men's shoes. This not only gave them the chance to marry, as we have already seen at Givry, but also took them out of the pool of labour. There was also an enormous increase in population mobility, which was already fairly considerable because of the previous excess of men over tenancies or jobs. Men rushed from the countryside into the towns. For example at Albi, in southern France, tax returns of 1343 before the first wave of plague suggest that the city then had some 10 700 inhabitants. The next tax returns, those of 1357, show that its population had dropped to some 4800 inhabitants, and, interestingly for our present purposes, that some forty-nine per cent of the inhabitants of one ward of the town were newcomers. Other towns in southern France, like Millau, show this same influx of newcomers, but so do towns as far away as Lubeck on the Baltic. This movement from country to town also reduced the pool of rural labour, although it increased that in the towns. The attempts to restrict wages by legislation, such as that by the Statute of Labourers in England, were almost totally ineffective, as only a few peasants or unpopular ecclesiastics were caught paying high wages to their hired hands. Wages continued to rise after successive waves of plague, although not so rapidly as after the first. Taken into conjunction with the fall in the price of basic foodstuffs, this meant that the diminishing numbers of wage labourers were able with their wages to buy a very great deal more than their ancestors.

242   The day-wages of master masons at Louvain in Brabant (now Belgium) reached their high point between 1442 and 1475. They could then have bought

over ten litres of Rhine wine a day with their wages, whereas their predecessors in the 1370s could have bought less than five litres. The bishop of Winchester's rural estate labourers between 1440 and 1459 could buy 136 per cent more corn with their wages than their predecessors between 1300 and 1319. With their additional purchasing power, labourers did not just buy more and more bread grain, or more and more wine (or beer depending on the part of Europe), they improved the quality of their life by buying semi-luxuries like meat and butter that their ancestors in a period of over-population could not have afforded. The rise in meat consumption not unexpectedly brought about a rise in meat prices, whereas wheat prices tended to fall. Indeed, surprisingly, much meat was eaten in the fifteenth century. At Carpentras in Provence in 1473 the average consumption of meat, apart from horseflesh, salt pork and game, reached 26 kilograms per head. This is much more than in France in the 1830s and 1840s, and that level of consumption was exceeded only quite late in the nineteenth century. In Spain and Greece that sort of consumption was only reached in the 1960s. It has been suggested that the standard of living purchasable by skilled workmen in the building trades in the 1470s was not reached again for almost exactly four hundred years.

Falling rents and abandoned land

243 Town rents plummeted after the first wave of plague, but rural rents moved more slowly. At least they stopped rising, but it was not until three waves of plague had removed the super-abundance of population that landlords really had to start competing to get tenants for their lands or face the prospect of their being untenanted. Rents went on falling until the 1470s on the lands of the abbey of St Germain des Pres, south of Paris. In 1350 the average rent per arpent had been 84 deniers. In the 1470s it was down to 31 deniers, a little over a third of the amount in money terms, and a great deal less than that in real terms, since the French coinage had considerably declined in value in between.

244 But even at dropping and attractive rents much of the marginal land that had been taken in under the population pressure of the thirteenth century went out of cultivation again. Abandonment of cultivated land took the place of reclamation of uncultivated land. In Languedoc the garrigues again became desolate, the assiduously drained flatlands along the coast reverted to salty swamp, whilst the oak forests that had been driven back in the Cevennes took over once more from the plough. Throughout Europe it was the same but in different degrees. In some places fields were abandoned, in others whole villages, even whole groups of villages. In densely inhabited Tuscany only ten per cent of the villages disappeared. Around Rome a quarter of the villages vanished. In Apulia perhaps as many as forty per cent. In parts of Germany, including some of the great settlement areas of the thirteenth century like Brandenburg, the desertion was as great. In Sardinia only half the villages were left. Some of this desertion took place after a single wave of plague, some of it even before but most of it happened in the fifteenth century after many waves of plague had reduced the population to the point at which the survivors had found themselves too few to form a viable community and had moved away, leaving the land to become forest and heath and swamp once more. Sometimes a solitary farm remained, trying to make the best of what was left. Sometimes a landlord, seeing his rent roll vanishing to nothing, made the best of a bad job by converting from arable to animal husbandry, to sheep in Midland England or Apulia, to cattle in Denmark or Hungary. Quite patently the scope for exploitation by the landlords had become minimal. It was the peasant who

could demand the land on his terms. The tenants who revolted in England in 1381 asking for rents of 4 pence an acre and the abolition of the remnants of villeinage may not have got what they wanted, but their grandchildren did. Rents dropped, and serfdom withered away in the fifteenth century, where it had not already been sold out of existence at a fat price in the thirteenth century.

245   The lowest point of population, like the highest point, arrived at different dates in different parts of Europe; indeed in a few places, like Flanders and Brabant, or the duchy of Milan, the population remained relatively high. In consequence they appeared as islands of high rents, high prices and low wages.

Fall in landed incomes and noble reaction

246   How did the depression in population affect the nobility? Quite obviously their incomes dropped catastrophically. Empty lands produced nothing: lands converted to sheep or cattle produced much less than when they had been teeming with rack-rentable peasantry, and those still occupied by peasant tenant-farmers produced lower rents and little or nothing in perquisites. Demesne farming, where it had survived on wage labour, was abandoned because of the rise in price of labour, and the land turned over to tenants, if they could be found. This meant an enormous overall drop in noble incomes. We can illustrate this best by comparing over a period the incomes of ecclesiastical estates which stayed about the same size. The landed income of the bishops of Durham sank by three-quarters, from £4526 sterling in 1308 to £1144 sterling in 1446. That of the bishops of Pamiers, in an area of southern France much devastated by war, fell over the same period by seven-eighths, from around £4000 tournois to around £500 tournois. We have no comparable figures for lay noble estates. Lay noblemen took aggressive measures to keep their incomes up. The key means by which landlords could keep up their family incomes was to negotiate successful marriages to landed heiresses, so that even if incomes fell from every particular area of land, the total family income was still maintained, or even increased, by radically increasing the area of land owned. This sort of aggressive heiress hunting, pursued over the generations by such families as the Bourbons in France or the Nevilles in England, meant that there was a rapid and deliberate thinning out of the nobility from the early fourteenth century to the late fifteenth century.

247   From being a wide social group, nobility became a narrow hierarchy. The same seems to have happened in a great variety of countries in this period. A few very rich families succeeded to a much wider group of less rich families. It has been estimated that an undifferentiated mass of some three thousand noble families in England in 1300 gave way to a small aristocracy of some sixty great families by 1500, with hereditary titles, separated by great wealth from a much poorer group of gentry. In Castille a handful of rich *grandees* emerged, and an impoverished mass of *hidalgos*. These very few, very rich men may not have had anything like the total purchasing power of their wide range of ancestors, but individually they could exert considerable patronage. For example the Duke of Berry was able to afford a prestigious library and employ the Limburg brothers to illuminate his manuscripts (see Unit 3, p. 25) and the Duke of Anjou was able to employ the goldsmith Gusmin whose work was so much admired by Ghiberti. Court circles then continued through this period, their members being many fewer, but individually richer than before. The court circle of Richard II was dominated by a handful of extremely rich men, of whom the Duke of Lancaster was the richest. It was in this milieu that

Chaucer wrote, with a salary from the king, and the patronage of the Duke of
Lancaster, for whom he wrote 'The Book of the Duchess'.

248   What of the bottom end of the noble class in this period of economic depression
and low population? The gentry in England, the *hidalgos* in Spain, the *petit
noblesse* in France, were affected in just the same way as the great landlords by
the dropping of their rent rolls. They had to struggle to keep their heads above
water and they found it practically impossible to keep up any sort of 'gentle'
existence on their lands alone. Some were reduced to farming themselves,
reducing themselves to the level of the richer peasantry, and ceasing to live a
'gentle' life. Others, in order to keep up that standard of living, had to borrow
heavily from townsfolk, and consequently lost their status after a short time
by debt, mortgage and eventual sale of their lands to people of urban origin,
who formed a new group of rural landowners. Many managed to maintain
themselves by the profits of that most 'gentle' of all occupations, war-making,
for which ample opportunities existed. This was the century of the Hundred
Years War, of the great wars between the city states in Italy, of civil wars in
Spain, of civil wars throughout Germany, and even in England, at the end of
this period, of the Wars of the Roses.

249   Froissart[1] sketched one such man, of gentle origin, whose predicament was
typical of the 1350s and 1360s:

> Among those who came to the Count's court I met a Gascon squire called the
> Bascot de Mauleon, a man of about fifty-five with the appearance of a bold and
> experienced soldier. He arrived with plenty of followers and baggage at the
> hostelry where I was staying at Orthez... He had as many packhorses with
> him as any great baron, and he and his people took their meals off silver plate.
> (p. 280.)

The Bascot described his origins briefly to Froissart:

> I have always held the frontier and fought for the King of England, for my
> family estate lies in the Bordeaux district. Sometimes I have been so thoroughly
> down that I hadn't even a horse to ride, and at other times fairly rich, as luck
> came and went. (p. 288.)

250   Froissart gives a horrifyingly vivid picture of men like this milling round
France making a living from pillaging and brigandage, after the official peace
of 1360, and eventually holding the pope and cardinals to ransom at Avignon,
before some of them were siphoned off to Italy:

> When this peace was concluded, one of its conditions was that all fighting-men
> and companions-in-arms must clear out of the forts and castles they held. *So
> large numbers of poor companions trained in war came out and collected together.* Some of
> the leaders held a conference about where they should go, and they said that,
> *though the kings had made peace, they had to live somehow.* They went to Burgundy
> and they had captains of all nationalities, English, Gascons, Spaniards,
> Navarrese, Germans, Scots and men from every country, and I was there as a
> captain. There were more than twelve thousand of us in Burgundy and along the
> Loire, counting everyone.

> And I tell you that in that assembly there were three or four thousand really
> fine soldiers, as trained and skilled in war as any man could be, wonderful men
> at planning a battle and seizing the advantage, at scaling and assaulting towns
> and castles, as expert and experienced as you could ask for... They all grew
> rich on good prisoners and the towns and fortresses they took in the arch-
> bishopric of Lyons and down the Rhone. The crowning touch to the campaign
> was the capture of Pont-Saint-Esprit, for then they made war on the Pope and
> the Cardinals and really made them squeal. They could not get rid of them,
> and never would have done until everything had been destroyed if they had not
> thought of a way out. They sent to Lombardy to invite the Marquis of Mont-
> ferrat, who was at war with the lord of Milan. When he reached Avignon the
> Pope and cardinals made an agreement with him and he talked to the English,

[1] Froissart, *Chronicles*, trans. G. Brereton, Penguin, Harmondsworth 1968 (pp. 282–3)

Gascon and German captains. On payment of sixty thousand francs by the Pope and the cardinals, several captains of companies, such as Sir John Hawkwood, a fine English knight . . . and several others gave up Pont-Saint-Esprit and *went off to Lombardy, taking three-fifths of all the men with them*. But we stayed behind. . . We had . . . more than sixty forts in the Maconnais, in Forez, Velay, Lower Burgundy and on the Loire, and we held the whole country to ransom. *They couldn't get rid of us, either by paying us good money, or otherwise.*

Impotence of central government and shrinkage of towns

251   Whilst the nobility and gentry of Europe were struggling to keep up their standards of living, despite their falling rent-rolls, their rulers were in no better plight. Their tax incomes fell, partly because of the general collapse of landed incomes, but also because their greater subjects appropriated or mis-appropriated the state revenues to their own use. In this way the already declining revenues of the Kings of France were further reduced when they were diverted to the treasuries of the Dukes of Orleans and Berry, Brittany and Bourbon. Other rulers, from the Kings of Naples and of Castille to the Kings of England and the margraves of Brandenburg suffered in the same way, and a limited number of their courts became less those of their rulers than of their greater subjects. The patronage exercised by the Duke of Lancaster at the court of Richard II of England (1377–99) or by the Dukes of Anjou and of Berry at the court of Charles VI of France (1380–1422) depended in part on their possession of royal revenues as well as income from their own landed property. France began to fall to pieces and the greater nobility to act like semi-autonomous princes with their own miniature courts and capitals. They too had chanceries and exchequers. Some of them even founded universities, like those at Nantes (Brittany) and Bourges (Berry) to supply themselves with civil servants. The royal orders of chivalry such as the Garter (England) or the Star (France), were imitated by these dukes to build up their circles of patronage. The Dukes of Orleans had the Order of the Porcupine, and the Dukes of Bourbon the improbably named Order of the Shackle (fer de prisonnier).

252   However, the two areas of Europe with a population that remained high, the Po Valley and the area now occupied by the 'Benelux' countries had not only atypically high rents, high prices and low wages, and consequently a broadly based and generally wealthy nobility, but also strong governments. In the late fourteenth and early fifteenth centuries the Dukes of Burgundy accumulated the rule of most of the 'Benelux' area, whilst the Visconti rulers of Milan dominated much of Lombardy. The Estense and Gonzagas consolidated their rule in Mantua and Ferrara. In the mid-fifteenth century Philip Duke of Burgundy was almost certainly the richest ruler in Europe, with a greater income than the impoverished kings of France or England. The type of extravagant luxury that the court of Burgundy could afford is an extreme example of this kind of development. Philip could also afford to support the new university of Louvain and such notable painters as Van Eyck and van der Weyden. The great men of the Burgundian state, led by the Chancellor Rolin, and the 'finance minister' Bladelin added their patronage to the galaxy of artists of the fifteenth-century Netherlands, as did the greatest of the merchants who purveyed luxury goods to the court, like Arnolfini from Lucca or Portinari from Florence.

253   The Visconti ducal capital of Milan was possibly the largest city in mid-fifteenth-century Europe, possibly even surpassing Paris in population. These were, however, islands in a sea of contracting governments throughout the rest of Europe.

254   The purchasing power of governments and of the nobility in general, was much reduced in the later fourteenth century and still more in most of the fifteenth century. However, as these shrinking landlord incomes were in fewer and fewer hands, whilst there was a reduced overall demand for luxuries, it was concentrated at the most luxurious end of the production range. The woollen cloth manufacture in Flanders and Brabant very noticeably shrank in scale, but the traditional textile towns of Ghent and Ypres went on producing cloths of the very highest quality for the small luxury market, while the surrounding small centres produced a much poorer article for 'yeoman' consumption. In Tuscany the same thing happened. The highest quality woollen cloth went on being produced in much reduced quantities, and only the top end of luxury manufacture, of silk, and cloth of gold, expanded. In Professor Hilton's broadcast, as well as in Unit 7, you will find a discussion of the nature and effects of this economic depression, and even a discussion of to what extent there was a 'depression' at all.

255   Certainly the multi-branched international business firm with all the necessary commercial techniques for its successful operation did not go out of existence. The commercial revolution was not undone, even though the scale of business shrank enormously. Many of these Italian-based international companies, even the biggest, went bankrupt in the 1340s, others in the 1370s, and yet others in the 1460s on the eve of economic revival.

256   A glance at the table of town populations (see para. 266) will show that whilst the populations both of capital cities and of commercial and industrial cities did shrink, they did not shrink quite as much as the overall populations.

257   You will see that the one commercial city which really kept its prosperity and size was Venice, the key port and commercial focal point for the still prospering Lombardy and the Po Valley. Doge Mocenigo of Venice in 1423, in warning his co-citizens not to ruin their prosperity by war, spoke of Lombardy as the garden of Venice. What you will not see are the names of Brussels and Antwerp on the table, since, despite their rapid growth, their overall size did not yet bring them into the bottom category. Brussels became the capital of the Burgundian 'state' in the 1450s and Antwerp was growing at the same time to replace Bruges as the principal port of this 'kingdom'.

258   It is one of the paradoxes of history that the great Renaissance expenditure on 'culture' should have begun in the early fifteenth century when the overall resources of states and the nobility were approaching their lowest point. The places that could act as centres of Renaissance patronage in the early fifteenth century were all in Lombardy and the Low Countries, where population changes were atypical. Their spending power in a period of shrinkage can be simply explained in this way. The exception is Florence which is dealt with in Unit 7. It is worth bearing in mind that Florentine spending power on 'culture' was peculiar and needs accounting for when you consider the city, since its prosperity is not easily explained in general terms. The islands of prosperity surviving in the general decay do much to explain the area in which the various phenomena which historians and art historians choose to call the Renaissance first appeared. The timing of these phenomena may well be related to the interlude of relative peace from the death of Gian Galeazzo Visconti in 1402 to the re-opening of hostilities between Milan, Florence and Venice in 1423, when the resources of Florentines, Mantuans and Ferrarese were not tied up in war-expenditure, but could be spent on 'culture'.

259   The difference that peace and war could make to patronage is readily illustrated by the case of Alfonso of Aragon, Sicily and Naples, one of Vespasiano's key figures (see para. 204). For the first thirty years of his reign he was more or less

continuously engaged in the costly business of war, and it was only in the last decade or so of it that he had the spare spending power to earn the reputation of a Mycaenas. Federigo of Montefeltro, another of Vespasiano's key figures, made his career as a great mercenary, like Sir John Hawkwood (see para. 250), but went further, for he was an independent prince in his own right. After the peace of Lodi in 1454, Montefeltro was paid *not* to fight. He was paid a retainer of 60 000 ducats a year by Milan in peace, with the promise of 80 000 if war broke out. It is said that between 1468 and his death in 1482 he disposed of a clear income, after all his military and other expenses had been paid, of 50 000 ducats a year, which was probably more pocket money than any other ruler in Western Europe. This very superior thug, by now Duke of Urbino, chose to spend his profits of war on the arts. Besides building two notable palaces at Urbino and Gubbio, he built up an enormous manuscript library (he was one of Vespasiano's best customers), attracted to himself a German astrologer and a Greek philologist to teach his son, and employed two of the most notable painters of his generation; the Italian Piero della Francesca and the Flemish Justus of Ghent. The latter, for example, painted the portrait of the duke and his son listening to a humanist oration as the centrepiece of a set of paintings on the seven liberal arts in his study at Gubbio. The painting of the duke is now at Hampton Court, and two of the seven liberal arts are in the National Gallery in London. This military entrepreneur behaved like an ideal renaissance prince, and Castiglione set *The Courtier* in the court of his son.

QUESTIONS

260 Answer the following questions for your own satisfaction. If you cannot do so look back and check.

1 Why was more than one wave of plague necessary to reverse population growth?

2 How did rents, prices, and wages normally react to dropping population in a pre-industrial economy?

3 How did noble incomes react to falling population?

4 Did the numbers of the nobility increase or decrease between 1320 and 1470?

5 Were the remaining nobility more, or less prosperous?

6 How did 'the gentry' respond to their economic situation?

7 Why did rulers become less powerful in the fourteenth century?

8 Which two areas of Europe had relatively high population and strong government in the fifteenth century?

9 Who would support spending on the arts in the early 'renaissance' in a period of 'economic decline'? Find examples of the types of patron available.

Now look at the relevant parts of the set book. Denys Hay (1966) *Europe in the Fourteenth and Fifteenth Centuries*, to amplify this section. It will also amplify your answers to some, but not all, of these questions. Note that some of Hay's emphases are different from ours. He writes about the peasantry in this period on pp. 27–38; the nobility and gentry on pp. 60–70; towns and trade on pp. 71–7 and on 359–393. Some of this you will notice is more relevant to our earlier section on the 'Long Thirteenth Century'.

THE LONG SIXTEENTH CENTURY OF THE PRICE REVOLUTION

Population growth

261   There was no cessation of the plague waves in the fifteenth century, or in the sixteenth, or indeed until the eighteenth century when the 1709–13 wave suddenly petered out and brought the series to an abrupt end. The intensity of the plague waves seems to have been milder and their extent more limited, sufficiently so at any rate for the natural tendency of human populations to grow to be able to reassert itself. We shall not deal at length with population growth here since it is admirably covered in pp. 28–32 of the set book by H. Koenigsberger and G. Mosse.

Rising prices, falling real wages and rising rents

262   From 1460 or so, prices of foodstuffs began to rise again, wages in consequence began to buy less and less, rents began to creep up, deserted lands began to be resettled, although not always exactly as before. Conditions became better for the landlord and worse for the tenant. In Eastern Germany and the neighbouring lands, an area that had been notable for its frontier freedom in the previous period of expansion, the landlords imposed a second serfdom on the descendants of these free settlers. In England, which had been noticeably backward in the thirteenth century, the prosperous peasantry of the fifteenth century who had accumulated several former family holdings in the period of population decline passed on their consolidated farms to their yeomen descendants in the sixteenth century. The latter, although paying increasing rents to their landlords, kept up with the price rise by selling the needed agricultural produce on the market and eased out the husbandmen who could not quite keep up with the price rise, adding their holdings to their own, and reducing their descendants to labourers, who inhabited the attics of the big new yeoman farmhouses built in late Elizabethan England. In France, on the other hand, the same prosperous peasantry of the fifteenth century did not pass their land on intact to their descendants, but divided it again and again amongst their heirs, so that the atomization of peasant holdings in France by the late sixteenth century somewhat resembled that in the early fourteenth and peasant conditions markedly deteriorated to the advantage of the landlords. In northern Italy it was altogether different. In the late thirteenth and early fourteenth century an effect of inflation was to drive landlords away from leasing for money, even for short terms of years, and to engage in *mezzadria*, share-cropping leases, in which the landlord and the tenant shared the proceeds of exploiting the land between them. For such a method to work at all efficiently, it had to be done on a moderately large scale, and holdings were deliberately amalgamated by the lords to form *poderes*, farms half of whose produce was enough to support one family. These two-family-sized farms remained largely un-amalgamated through the period of population decline (where they were not abandoned), and undivided through the period of increased poplulation. Many of them seem to have remained unchanged until the nineteenth century.

Rise in landed incomes and of the gentry

263   The revived prosperity of landlords, now that more land was again under cultivation and higher rents could be demanded, particularly affected the

lower ranks of the nobility. The descendants of such men as the Bascot of Mauleon could again live on their rent rolls in a 'gentle' way. They no longer had to resort to stratagems to survive. The sixteenth century 'rise of the gentry' marked the re-emergence of the group who had suffered most in the preceding 'depression'. Such men could now rebuild their manor houses, send their sons to university, and buy a wide range of the less expensive luxuries, including new ones such as printed books. The reviving and increasing purchasing power of the English gentry, the Spanish hidalgos, the petite noblesse of France and the junkers of Prussia, set in train a vast revival and extension of international trade in these less expensive luxuries.

artifice in war; trick, device

Renewal of government, taxation, and growth of capital cities

264   As central governments from the second half of the fifteenth century onwards became more efficient under such rulers as Edward IV in England, Louis XI in France and Ferdinand and Isabella in Aragon and Castille, and as powers which had been 'usurped' by lesser rulers, such as the Dukes of Berry or Anjou were re-absorbed into 'national' governments, the revenues of monarchies enormously increased. A more than thirty-fold increase in the royal revenues of Castile during the reign of Isabella brought her income at the end of her reign back to those of her predecessors before the catastrophic drop in revenue. It was not, however, only the re-absorption of lesser 'governments', and the increase in efficiency of collection which made the difference, but also the enormous increase in taxable capacity. In a very real sense the wealth of the princes did depend on the wealth of their subjects. The healthily revived revenues of Isabella depended primarily on the alcalala, a tax on internal sales; that of Edward IV and Henry VII on the customs on overseas sales; that of Louis XI on the taille, primarily a land tax bearing on the peasantry; that of Manuel of Portugal on taxes on the spice trade with India, which earned him the soubriquet from Francis I of France, 'Le Roi Epicier' (the Grocer King).

265   The chart of cities (para. 266) shows how the capital cities reacted to the growth in wealth and political organization of their rulers. Old capitals like Paris and Naples (the headquarters of Ferdinand of Aragon for his Italian dominions) shot up in size in the second half of the fifteenth century and went on growing in the sixteenth century, with Tudor London and the Rome of the Renaissance and counter-reformation Papacy not so very far behind.

266   *The Capital Cities of Western Europe*

	1300	1400	1500	1600
200 000 to 400 000				Naples
				Paris
100 000 to 200 000			Naples	London
			Paris	Rome
			Milan	Lisbon
				Milan
				Venice
60 000 to 100 000	Paris	Milan		Madrid
	Milan	Paris		
c. 50 000	Naples	Naples	Lisbon	Brussels
	London		Rome	Vienna
	Palermo		London	Prague
	Rome			

The Commercial and Industrial Cities

200 000 to 400 000				None
100 000 to 200 000			Venice	Seville Amsterdam
60 000 to 100 000	Venice Florence Genoa	Venice	Cordoba Seville Granada Florence Genoa	9 cities including Florence Genoa Lyons Antwerp
c. 50 000	Ghent	Florence Genoa	12 cities including Lyons Ghent Antwerp	17 cities including Leyden Haarlem

(Adapted from Mols, R. (1954–6) *Introduction á la Demographie Historique des Villes d'Europe.*)

They were joined by the Grocer King's capital at Lisbon, which remained among the top handful of cities until Portugal was absorbed by Spain. The fastest capital growth in the sixteenth century was in Philip II's Madrid. Whereas his father, the Emperor Charles V, had spent his lifetime on the road between his various dominions, Philip II decided that he could most efficiently rule his dominions from one place and accordingly built his palace-monastery of the Escorial outside the medium-sized Castillian city of Madrid. There had been no capital at all in mediaeval Castille. Unlike most thirteenth-century monarchs, those of Castille did not stop moving about. Italian observers were astonished by the speed with which Madrid grew and by the contrast between the luxurious palaces built by the grandees and the vast shanty town around which poverty-stricken bands of hopeful migrants to the city lived, in conditions worse than stables in Italy.

267 Botero aptly sums up the focusing power of the capital cities in his day (he was writing in the 1580s):

> It doth infinitely avail to the magnifying and making cities great and populous the residency of the prince therein according to the greatness of whose empire she does increase for where the prince is resident, there also the parliaments are held, and the supreme place of justice is there kept. All matters of importance have recourse to that place, all princes and all persons of account, ambassadors of princes and of commonwealths, and all agents of cities that are subject make their repair thither; all such as aspire and thirst after offices and honours rush thither amain with emulation and disdain for others. Thither are the revenues brought that pertain unto the state, and there are they disposed of again.
> (Giovanni Botero (1588) *Of the Greatness of Cities.*)

And besides this, the reviving estate revenues of the landlords were focused on these capital cities.

The renewal of commerce

268 To these focal points the revived commerce of the long sixteenth century was directed. The combined and growing demand of royalty and nobility in these cities was the motor of the revival and growth of international trade. The key markets of Europe in 1600 were the capitals, just as they had been in 1300.

Just as the initial focusing of trade on certain routes in the thirteenth and early fourteenth centuries had brought the volume of trade to a level which allowed the qualitative changes in commercial techniques summed up in the term 'commercial revolution', so now the re-focusing of expanding trade brought the quantity of trade above that critical threshold in new places. The rapid growth of Antwerp, for example, was accompanied by the extension of Italian commercial techniques not only to Antwerp itself, but to the south German cities like Nuremburg and Augsberg. These contained the head offices of some of the multi-branched business firms, like the Fuggers and the Welsers, who dominated the Antwerp market. They had interests ranging from the exploitation of mercury in Andalusia to the exploitation of copper in Hungary, from the trade in sugar and spices and cloth at Antwerp to the manufacture of iron in Thuringia and the mining of silver in the Tirol.

269   In the early sixteenth century the cloth trade of Europe was focused on Antwerp, but the great textile manufacturing centres were now at Ghent and Honschoote, whilst by the end of the sixteenth century the centre of the cloth trade had moved to Amsterdam and that of textile manufacture to nearby Haarlem and Leyden. When the industrial centres were in different places from the commercial centres it is easier to see the hierarchy of cities, from capital cities through commercial cities to industrial ones, with the vast mass of small towns throughout Europe combining the functions of local administrative centres, as county towns; of local commerce, as market towns; and of small scale craftsmanship to meet local demand.

270   It is fascinating to see how the demand focused in these capital cities had cultural as well as material luxury content. The same aristocratic markets that consumed sugar also consumed books, and centres of sugar refining were also centres of printing. When, in the late fifteenth century, Venice was the key point for sugar refining, as well as of the copper and spice trades, it became the focal point for printing for the Europe-wide élite market. It was here that Aldus Manutius had the most prestigious, and prolific, printing house in Europe in 1500. A generation later, sugar refining, and the spice and copper trades were focused on Antwerp, and Antwerp became in its turn the focal point for printing. It was here that Plantin had his famous printing house. By the end of the century Amsterdam had taken over the commercial role of Antwerp, and Elzevier of Amsterdam was the principal publisher to the nobility and gentry of Europe.

271   Now this may seem a very long way from the peasant at the bottom of society. But we would maintain that it depended very much upon the relationship between men and land, whether the upper classes, from the gentry through the upper nobility to the ruler or prince, were in a position to make demands on the peasantry, to take the surplus of their labour and their land; and that it is in times like the thirteenth century and again the sixteenth century, when there is overcrowding and overpopulation in the countryside, that it is possible for a great surplus to be taken; whereas at times between the mid-fourteenth and the mid-fifteenth century, when the population was much lower, there was much less. Thus, in the thirteenth century and again in the sixteenth, there was a strengthening of the state and a great increase in its power, an extension of the machinery of government and a growth of capital cities. Paris, Westminster and Naples so developed for the first time in the thirteenth century, and there was another growth, sometimes a re-growth of capital cities in the sixteenth century. In these capitals we find the focus of patronage and of growth in civilizations.

QUESTIONS

272   Answer the following questions for your satisfaction. If you cannot do so look back and check.

1   How did rents, prices and wages normally react to rising population in a pre-industrial economy?

2   Did the prosperity of landlords generally rise or fall with the increased population?

3   Why did the incomes of governments increase in the sixteenth century?

4   Look up the present populations of your nearest market, county and industrial towns and compare them with the size of capital, commercial and industrial cities between 1300 and 1600.

5   We have suggested that the 'renaissance' was a movement that only affected elite social groups, and the patronage they offered. Use your own common sense to consider whether the Reformation is likely to have been socially confined in the same way. The patronage and protection of rulers and noblemen was likely to be as important to Reformation beliefs as to renaissance art, but there was one crucial difference. Humble men and women were sometimes prepared to die for their beliefs, but never for art. We have not given you an answer to this question and part of the answer depends on facts about basic literacy rates which are not available to you. We would like you to bear the question in mind just the same until you get to units 20 and 27.

Now look at the relevant parts of the set book, H. G. Koenigsberger and George L. Mosse (1968) *Europe in the Sixteenth Century*, to amplify this section. They write about prices and population on pp. 21–45, and trade and towns on pp. 45–83. You may like to miss out some, but not all, of the examples between pages 59 and 73, but you should look at the end pp. 73–83.

PART 3   THE LATE MEDIAEVAL WORLD PICTURE

by Noel Coley

CONTENTS

Introduction   83

Late Mediaeval Cosmography   84

    Substance and accident; matter and form   85
    The potential and the actual   85
    Natural and forced motion   86
    The void   87
    Cause and purpose   88
    The doctrine of the four elements   89
    Plato's influence on cosmography, the *Timaeus* 89
    The harmony of the spheres   92
    Neo-Platonism   94

INTRODUCTION

300   Natural phenomena continually occur all about us, yet we do not commonly give them a second thought except perhaps to grumble when the weather is bad. Day follows night in regular succession, the moon waxes and wanes, the sun rises in the east. We can even take the unusual or catastrophic phenomenon in our stride. For example the appearance of a comet is a matter both of general interest and for scientific study, but not, as it once was, for superstitious fear. We no longer regard the comet as a portent of disaster, a messenger from God, for we know that there is a rational, scientific explanation, although we ourselves may not be capable of understanding it in full. Nevertheless we have all heard of radiation and the electron and are vaguely aware that atomic energy provides the light and other radiations of the stars. X-rays and radio-activity, too, are familiar terms to most people and we know that there are many stars which although invisible to the eye, can be detected by means of the radio telescope. We can also accept the idea that the universe is virtually infinite and is expanding all the time. These and other concepts find their way into our thinking from our lessons at school, or through the press, radio and television; they have become part of our modern description of the world. But if we carry this twentieth-century world picture into our Renaissance studies without modification we shall inevitably make for ourselves difficulties of interpretation.

301   The framework within which mediaeval thought developed was provided by the Christian faith, and the idea that reasoning must remain in conformity with the dictates of faith is central to mediaeval thinking. But this exclusive allegiance to a defined body of dogma did not mean that there was *uniformity* of thought. Mediaeval people drew their ideas from a number of sources in addition to the Bible and the fathers of the early Church. Mediaeval thought was influenced by Greek philosophy, particularly the systems of Plato and Aristotle; Neo-Platonism as developed in the third and fourth centuries AD and the systems of Arabian and Jewish thinkers of the tenth, eleventh and twelfth centuries. There was, in addition, a smattering of Greek and Arabian science. These influences were not equal in importance, nor did they all reach the west at the same time. They mingled uneasily, forming a changing multitude of ideas, so that mediaeval thought was every bit as complex as that of any other period in history.

302   In every age, man's description of the world is integrated into his beliefs, and finds both explicit and implicit expression in his art and literature. Read Thomas Middleton's idea of wisdom and knowledge in 'The Wisdom of Solomon Paraphrased', (*Penguin Book of Elizabethan Verse*, p. 193). What does it tell us about the world picture of its time?

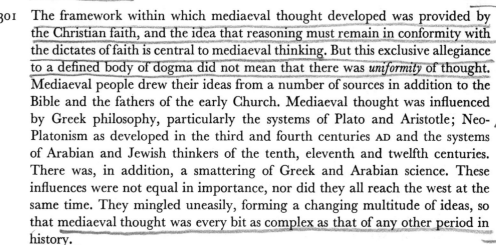

303   *Suggested Answer*
In Middleton's knowledge of the world, natural forces and events are explained in terms which show the influence of Aristotelian and Platonic doctrines. Thus the motions of stars and the heavenly spheres mark out time – the seasons and the climates. There is recognition of the unique qualities of every created thing, and a hint of the medicinal values of plants. But with all this empirical observation, true knowledge is to be obtained by 'wit' and reasoning in the classic Platonic tradition.

But in order to understand poems like this one it is clear that we need to make a conscious effort to put aside our modern world picture and take up that of the late Middle Ages.

LATE MEDIAEVAL COSMOGRAPHY

304   To the educated observer of the fifteenth century the universe appeared as an intelligible, explicable, closely interrelated whole. It was of finite size, limited by the sphere of the so-called 'fixed stars'. Everything which had a physical existence was contained within this sphere. Below the sphere of fixed stars were other spheres, concentric with each other and with the Earth, moving with endless, perfect, circular motions and carrying with them the other heavenly bodies (Sun, Moon, Mercury, Venus, Mars, Jupiter and Saturn).

305   Both the crystalline spheres and the heavenly bodies themselves were regarded as perfect, complete and incorruptible. They were even assigned a special element, unknown in the terrestrial region. This fifth element, or 'quintessence', was often considered to be entirely separate from the four terrestrial elements, though sometimes it was thought to have been distilled from them in exhalations which, rising from the Earth, ascended to nourish the stars and the Sun.

306   At the centre of all the circling spheres stood the immobile Earth, surrounded by the terrestrial region below the sphere of the Moon. Here everything was thought to be made up of mixtures of the four elementary principles: earth, fire, air and water;[1] motion was mainly in straight lines 'up' or 'down'; imperfection, temporal transience and corruptibility were commonplace. (See Unit 15, pp. 15–18.)

Can you suggest any reasons why the heavens should have been thought to be perfect?

307   *Suggested Answer*
In an age of naked eye astronomy, stars appeared like jewels, and planets, Moon and Sun seemed to be perfectly smooth; their motions appeared to be smooth since slight deviations were hard to detect. Observations of the heavens led directly to geometry, which in the Platonic tradition was the branch of knowledge which most nearly aspired to the realms of pure thought and reality. Thus the heavens could be seen as a physical expression of perfect reality and truth. Lastly, awe-inspiring events were sometimes seen to occur in the heavens, indicating immense power such as might be attributed to God.

308   Descriptions of entities and phenomena in the physical world were traditionally based on ancient authorities, especially Plato and Aristotle. Before the twelfth century Aristotle's works were virtually unknown in the west, although some of Plato's writings were available (including part of the *Timaeus*: see paras 332–8). Plato's approach to reality, with its emphasis on the need to transcend the physical world so as to reach the ideal and eternal, was broadly in accord with Christian thought, although Plato assigned no place to God in his system. Aristotle on the other hand, took an empirical view of the nature of existence and his analysis, unlike that of Plato, was concerned with things rather than ideas. The first Latin translations of Aristotle's works were drawn from Arabic sources, but later translations were taken directly from the Greek. (For further discussion of Plato and Aristotle see Unit 5 paras 5.1 to 5.4).

By the fifteenth century the teachings of Plato and Aristotle had become modified through the interpretative commentaries of numerous scholars and the incorporation of concepts derived from other Greek philosophers as well as ideas from Neo-Platonic, Arabian and Christian sources.

[1] NB Not the common substances of everyday experience but purified, 'metaphysical' forms of these entities.

Substance and accident; matter and form

309   For Aristotle, 'substance' denotes the being of every concrete, individual thing which exists; it is the most fundamental mode of being and may be distinguished from other categories of being such as quality, quantity, position etc. These latter categories are regarded as accidental modes of being. Now, whereas substances may exist in their own right, the existence of accidents is dependent upon the existence of substances in which they inhere. For example the accidents of the substance 'yourself' include your nationality (quality), your stature (quantity), your situation (place), and so on.

For Plato, things in the terrestrial world were but pale, imperfect reflections of the universal ideals, and reality was to be found only in the realm of pure forms or ideas. For him the path to reliable knowledge of the real world lay in the direction of abstract thought; the forms or ideas alone provided certainty. (Refer again to Unit 5, para. 5.1.) The study of mathematics (i.e. *geometry* for the Greeks), provided the best hope of achieving such knowledge of reality and this was the reason for the importance which Plato attached to this branch of study.

310   Aristotle distinguished between matter and form, but he denied that the real world was one of forms, and that the latter could have an existence independently of matter. For Aristotle, knowledge of the real world must begin with sense perception. Matter and form were inextricably blended in each 'substance' and could only be separated in an intellectual exercise. Form is the unifying, structure-defining principle; matter has the capacity to acquire structure. Form makes matter into substances, but only substances have *being*; for Aristotle matter cannot exist without form.

The potential and the actual

311   'The egg's ordain'd by nature, to that end:
        And is a chicken " in *potentia*" '
        (The Alchemist II, 3.133.)

There is a vast difference between what a substance is and what it might become. The ancients and mediaeval people distinguished between these two phases as between 'actual' and 'potential' being. For instance, an acorn is potentially an oak, though actually an acorn; a block of marble is potentially a statue. What is the underlying difference between these two kinds of potentiality? You may need to think carefully here, though the distinction is quite simple.
Attempt an answer before reading on.

312   *Answer*
The acorn contains *within itself* the power to grow into an oak tree and will do so given the appropriate conditions, but the block of marble can only be converted into a statue by the action of human hands and mind. Also the block of marble may become *any* statue the sculptor may wish to make it, but the acorn can only grow into an oak, it could not become a beech tree.

313   In every substance there exist various possible potential forms and the process by which each potential is realized is very important. The process of 'becoming', which Aristotle explained in a different sense from that of his teacher Plato,

is especially relevant in the ever-changing terrestrial world. In every case the process of change involved a kind of motion. You will encounter some further interesting facets of the development of this theme when you come to the study of Elizabethan poetry later in the course. (Unit 30 pp. 48–9; 69–72.)

314 A stone suspended at the top of a cliff or tower has a potential existence at the centre of the earth – its 'natural place'. When set free the stone moves with natural motion towards its natural place. So we see the stone fall downwards towards the Earth, and in the same way we see flames of fire move upwards as fire seeks *its* natural place just below the sphere of the Moon.

315 There are two ideas here fundamental to mediaeval Aristotelian cosmography, which were always tacitly assumed but are not easy for us to grasp. First, there is the assumption implied in the concept of natural place that inanimate substances recognize their natural place and move towards it when not under constraint. More generally we could say that every substance, whether conscious or inanimate has a tendency to act in accordance with its own nature. Secondly, we note that motion is fundamental to the process of becoming. For the Aristotelian, motion was itself a *process* which required a continuously acting cause and it also had a *purpose*. But our modern term 'motion' is quite inadequate to convey the full meaning of the concept of 'motus' which included besides change of position, or local motion, change from one form to another.

316 For the Aristotelian then, motion in this wider sense was the process by which that which existed *in potentia* was made actual; it was the way towards a change of form – whether 'substantial form', i.e. related to the essential properties of the substance, or 'accidental form', i.e. concerning those properties such as temperature or position in space, which might be changed without changing the substance itself. In all cases there had to be a continuous cause acting throughout the duration of the change.

317 How does the Aristotelian conception of local motion compare with present ideas?

Discussion

For us, although there are some imprecise applications of the term in common use, motion strictly applies only to the change in position of a body, relative to other bodies in space. Now this kind of motion is regarded in physics not as a process but as a *state* requiring no more explanation than the state of rest. A body will remain at rest or will continue to move uniformly in a straight line unless and until some constraint is imposed. It is not motion itself, but *change of motion* or change from rest to motion which needs a cause and any cause which acts continuously will bring about progressive *change* of motion, not steady motion as the Aristotelians held. Lastly, the motion of a falling stone, or of the Moon about the Earth has, for us, no discernible purpose and for us to enquire about the purpose of motion in all such cases would be meaningless.

Natural and forced motion

318 Now within this wide definition, local motion already had great importance. Quantitative changes occur by addition or removal of parts; by expansion or contraction of the body itself. Commonly too, qualitative changes were seen to be brought about by the meeting at a point in space of the body undergoing

the change and the agent causing the change. In the terrestrial region the elements air and fire were thought to possess levity since they were always seen to move upwards towards the sphere of the moon, whilst earth and water showed gravity as they moved downwards towards the centre of the universe. These movements are examples of *natural* motion. Bodies move in these ways when released from constraints, and the causes of natural motion are usually internal to the body itself. One result of such vertical motions must be the sorting out of the four elements into layers, with earth at the centre surrounded by water, air and fire in that order. In this way the perfect state would eventually be achieved; and once again motion is involved in the process of becoming.

319 Now it is clearly possible to impose motion on a body in a direction opposite to its natural motion and the body would then move with *forced* motion. It would continue to do so only so long as the external cause of this motion continued to act. Since forced motion was thought to be opposed to natural motion, Aristotle taught that a body could not move with both kinds of motion at the same instant.

Can you suggest any common kinds of terrestrial motion for which these ideas (a) seem to be a plausible explanation, (b) must cause difficulties?

320 *Discussion*

a   The motion of a bullock cart for example. The cart continues to move along the road only so long as the oxen go on pulling it. Thus a continuously acting cause produces the steady motion of the cart.

b   Projectile motion. Once the arrow has left the bow, or the stone the hand, what can be the continuing cause which gives rise to its flight? Aristotelians, following their master, held that it was the air itself, which, rushing from the front of the projectile to the rear, propelled it forward on its flight. In this way, the air became at once the propellant and the source of resistance to the flight of the projectile. Again the path of the arrow or stone appears to the eye as a smooth curve, yet if the projectile can have only natural *or* forced motion at each instant of time, it must actually be a series of very small steps.

321 In fact the interpretation of Aristotle's ideas about motion caused real problems for mediaeval commentators, and later, in the sixteenth century, for Copernicus and his supporters.

The void

322 Aristotle had set out to produce a physical science of qualities. In order to account for changes in the physical world, Greek atomists had found it necessary to postulate the existence of both matter (the atoms) and empty space (the void), but Aristotle could not accept the latter – the being of 'not being'. In fact for Aristotle space must be co-extensive with matter. His arguments against the existence of the void are interesting and instructive. Consider the following examples:

323 1   A limited void would presuppose an environment in which substances *might* be placed, but in which no substances are actually present. It would have to be a thing bounded or limited by whatever it excluded or included, and if that were possible it would necessarily exist. But since a void is essentially non-existent this would be a logical contradiction and a void is therefore inconceivable.

324   2   In a boundless void, all possibility of determining place and direction would be eliminated. No point is distinguishable from any other; no direction is preferred to any other. A body placed in such a void could be said neither to move nor to remain motionless since its place is undefined.

All this is irreconcilable with the Aristotelian concept of a limited universe providing a fixed frame of reference by which the place of every substance within it could be determined.

325   3   The speed of fall of a freely moving body was thought by Aristotle to be directly proportional to its weight and inversely proportional to the resistance of the medium. Thus a stone falls more rapidly in air than water. Now since a void would offer no resistance at all, a body falling in a void would move with *infinite* speed and would reach the end of its fall at the same instant that it left the starting point. Moreover all bodies whatever their weight would fall with the same instantaneous motion. A body cannot exist at two points in the same instant and therefore there can be no void.

326   Throughout the Middle Ages people remained generally convinced that Aristotle was right and that no void could exist in nature. The most familiar formulation of this idea is that nature has a horror of the void (*horror vacui*), 'nature abhors a vacuum'.

Cause and purpose

327   Nothing happens or exists in the Aristotelian world without its precise and identifiable cause.

Substantial causality was considered under four complementary aspects:

The material cause	—	matter
The formal cause	—	form or idea into which the matter is to be realized
The efficient cause	—	causative agents
The final cause	—	ultimate purpose and part of the general plan of the universe as a whole

(For further discussion see Unit 5, p. 41.)

328   In Aristotelian thought most things could be accounted for in terms of this system of causes, which includes the matter, the form and the purpose to be ascribed to every substance and event observable in the physical world. The formal and final causes direct the movement from becoming to being, whilst the efficient cause presupposes the impulse to set the process in motion. Aristotle also held that there must be a first cause – an unmoved mover which initiates each train of development.

As a simple diversion consider how this theory of causes might be applied to the production of a statue from a block of marble.

Discussion

The marble itself would be the material cause; the idea of the statue in the mind of the sculptor would be the formal cause; the efficient cause would be provided by the working skill of the sculptor and the tools he uses, whilst the final cause would be the motivating purpose or the function the statue is intended to fulfil.

The doctrine of the four elements

'Does not our lives consist of the four elements?'
(*Twelfth Night*, II.3.8.)

329   Explanation in the physical science of the Middle Ages was based largely upon the interaction of pairs of opposite qualities (hot, cold; rough, smooth; wet, dry; heavy, light; and so on). The material bearers of these qualities could then be regarded as explanatory principles in themselves. All substances in the terrestrial region were thought to be composed of mixtures of the four elementary principles, earth, air, fire and water, to each of which was assigned a pair of 'active' qualities by which its presence could be detected. The active qualities were so-called because they could be transmitted from one substance to another and to any mixture of the elementary principles. In practice *all* tangible substances were considered to contain at least two of the four elements; even those things which commonly bear the names of the elements themselves.

	HOT	COLD
MOIST	AIR	WATER
DRY	FIRE	EARTH

330   Now, since each of the active qualities appears as a property of two different elements, changes from one element to another may readily occur (although such transmutations are easiest between pairs of elements having a common property).

Figure 52

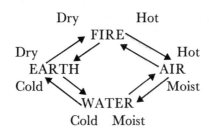

331   From the above it follows that all kinds of matter must ultimately be interconvertible and transmutations of every kind are possible given the appropriate conditions and the effective agents. For example, a mine producing metal ores which had been exhausted might well become productive again if left for long enough. The Earth, regarded as living, would nurture the growth of new ore from the rock in the mine. Again, the transmutation of base metals into gold was perfectly conceivable given the effective agents and conditions, and so the doctrine of the four elements provided a rational justification for the claims of alchemy. (See *The Alchemist*, II.3.140–75.)

Plato's influence on cosmography, the *Timaeus*

332   Although the physical theory of the Middle Ages had mainly been based on Aristotelian physics and philosophy, the influence of Platonic thought was never lost, but it should be emphasized that neither was present in the west in a sophisticated form until after the influx of Arabian science in the twelfth century and the rise of the universities. Many Platonic ideas found expression in the work of Aristotle, as, for instance, in the hierarchy of the heavenly spheres, the distinction between matter and form, and the conception of the universe as a living organism, although the last was specifically denied by

some mediaeval Aristotelian scholars including Thomas Aquinas. But Plato's influence can be traced more directly through the importance of his dialogue *Timaeus*, in which he gave an imaginative reasoned account of the creation of the universe and all that it contains, including man himself. The *Timaeus* first appeared in Athens about 348 BC and a part of it was translated into Latin by Chalcidius in the sixth century. In this form, together with another fragment translated by Cicero, the *Timaeus* survived through the Middle Ages, achieving immense importance in European thought.

333   This dialogue, or rather its first part, was studied and quoted throughout the Middle Ages, and there was hardly a mediaeval library of any standing which had not a copy of Chalcidius' version and sometimes also a copy of the fragment translated by Cicero. Although these facts are well known, their significance for the history of ideas has perhaps not been sufficiently grasped by historians. The *Timaeus* with its attempted synthesis of the religious teleological justification of the world and the rational exposition of creation was, throughout the earlier Middle Ages, the starting point and guide for the first groping efforts towards a scientific cosmology. Around this dialogue and the exposition of Chalcidius accompanying it in many manuscripts, there grew up an extensive literature of commentaries... The desire for a more rational explanation of the universe found its expression in the attempts to harmonize the Platonic and Mosaic narratives and to interpret the biblical account in Genesis by means of the Greek scientific categories and concepts which had become part of Western thought, mainly by way of the Latin *Timaeus* and its commentator. These tendencies culminated in the twelfth century in the School of Chartres which exercised a profound influence on the teachers of the arts in Paris in the following century...

334   The influence of the masters of Chartres ... revives in the doctrines of Nicholas of Cusa (1401–64) who, more perhaps than any other individual thinker, contributed to the formation of the so-called modern cosmology. This connexion between the Renaissance philosopher, in the judgement of contemporaries the 'grande Platoniste', and the Platonists of the twelfth century is a striking instance of the continuity of the Platonic tradition. Through Cusanus certain of their doctrines became known to Copernicus, as we are able to prove by the marginal notes in his copy of Bovillus' *Liber de intellectu*. The adherents of the 'Nova scientia', when they chose Plato as their guide in their fight against Aristotelianism, could take up the threads of a Platonic tradition which had never been entirely lost in the Latin world.

(R. Klibansky, *Continuity of the Platonic Tradition*, p. 28.)

335   Creation as described in the *Timaeus* involved a process of deliberate constructive activity, carried out by a divine craftsman. The construction of the heavens, the structure of terrestrial matter and human physiology are all discussed. The *Timaeus* influenced Neo-Platonists and its creator-god was easily assimilated into the Christian ethic.

336   The universe of the *Timaeus* consisted of a unique, perfect, self-contained sphere, revolving on its axis. It was suffused throughout and in all its parts with soul.

The universe as a whole was a living organism and man had been made in the image of the universe. This is the doctrine of the macrocosm and microcosm, from which are derived correspondences between the heavenly bodies and the various organs of the human body.

337   The *Timaeus* also gave expression to another general principle in keeping with the Platonic tradition, namely the importance of mathematics as a basis for all physical phenomena. A kind of geometrical atomism is described in which the fundamental units or atoms are minute triangles which are joined together so as to form particles in the regular (i.e. in which all the sides and all the angles are equal) shapes of the 'Platonic' solids (cube, tetrahedron, octahedron, icosahedron and dodecahedron – see Fig. 53).

Figure 53. The four elements and the regular solids according to Plato (Timaeus)

cube – earth   octahedron – air
tetrahedron – fire   icosahedron – water
The dodecahedron represents the cosmos

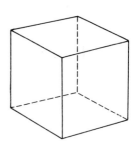

cube–earth

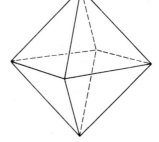

octahedron–air

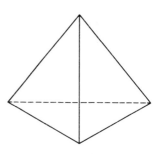

tetrahedron–fire

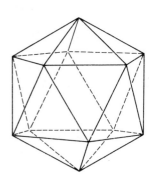

icosahedron–water

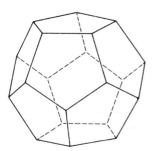

The dodecahedron represents the cosmos

It would, then, be possible to envisage transmutations between the elements simply by breaking down the particles of one element into its basic triangular units and recombining these again into the shapes of the particles of other elements.

338   In the world of the *Timaeus* there was a hierarchy of divine beings; astrologers who regarded the stars and heavenly bodies as divine could find the same sentiment in the *Timaeus* where the heavenly bodies were considered to be gods. Neo-Platonism, with its spiritual hierarchy could also look to the *Timaeus*, and so too could the hierarchies of Christian theology. In mediaeval times the generally accepted explanation of the origins of the world and of man himself was based on the Genesis account. Besides this the *Timaeus* is seen to be very esoteric – although the surviving fragment of it was widely known among scholars. You should bear these ideas in mind when you come to study Unit 11 on Iconography.

The harmony of the spheres

339   Plato's mathematical tendencies found expression in his treatment of the ordering of the heavenly spheres. Here too there was a hierarchy:

> For far above these heavens, which here we see,
> Be others far exceeding these in light,
> Not bounded, not corrupt, as these same be,
> But infinite in largeness and in height,
> Unmoving, uncorrupt, and spotless bright,
> That need no sun t'illuminate their spheres
> But their own native light far passing theirs.
> And as these heavens still by degrees arise
> Until they come to their first mover's bound,
> That in his mighty compass doth comprise
> And carry all the rest with him around;
> So those likewise do by degrees redound
> And rise more fair, till they at last arrive
> To the most fair, whereto they all do strive
>
> (E. Spenser, *Hymn of Heavenly Beauty* (Four Hymns: 1596))

340   These 'heavens', the spheres of the planets, were thought to be arranged in mathematical progression and as they turned they gave out musical notes the frequencies of which were related to the sizes and speeds of rotation of the different spheres. Pliny suggested that the musical scale of the spheres contained the following notes:

$$C \quad D \quad E\flat \quad E \quad G \quad A \quad B\flat \quad B \quad D$$

Earth ———————————————— Firmament

There were other possible variants, but in all cases the effect was one of an unimaginable, divinely beautiful sound. The idea that the universe was suffused by music can be traced back to the Pythagoreans. It was common in the mediaeval period; Isidore of Seville (c. 560–636), most popular of all mediaeval encyclopaedists, wrote:

> Nothing exists without music; for the universe itself is said to have been framed by a kind of harmony of sounds, and the heaven itself revolves under the tones of that harmony.

The notion was revived with the Platonic renaissance of the fifteenth century and it continued thereafter throughout the Elizabethan period. Thus Milton in 1629 could still write:

> Ring out ye Crystall sphears,
> Once bless our human ears,
> (If ye have power to touch our senses so)
> And let your silver chime
> Move in melodious time;
> And let the Bass of Heav'ns deep Organ blow,
> And with your ninefold harmony,
> Make up full consort to the Angelike symphony.
>
> (Milton, *On the Morning of Christ's Nativity, The Hymn*, (stanza XIII))

341   That the music of the spheres was never heard on earth was sometimes held to be due to the grossness of our ears though it might also be thought that it was not physical music at all but music of the soul.

> . . . Look how the floor of heaven
> Is thick inlaid with patines of bright gold;
> There's not the smallest orb which thou behold'st
> But in his motion like an angel sings,

> Still quiring to the young-eyed cherubims;
> Such harmony is in immortal souls;
> But whilst this muddy vesture of decay
> Doth grossly close it in, we cannot hear it.

(*Merchant of Venice*, Act V Sc. 1. (Poetry Anthology p. 222–3))

(But see Units 5/6, pp. 52–3, and Unit 30, pp. 63–68 for further work on this theme.)

342 The concept of the harmony of the spheres is another example of the fundamental importance of mathematics in the construction of the universe, although in this case it is applied in a mystical sense.

If you are interested in the detailed mathematical discussion of this musical theory and its relation to architecture you will find it in Wittkower (the set book for Unit 9).

343 Although the common framework of mediaeval thinking was provided by the Christian faith, regulated by the Church and largely sustained by ecclesiastics, many activities of an occult nature were also current owing to the influence of Arabian and Jewish occultists and to early Renaissance speculative Platonists (e.g. Pico della Mirandola – see Unit 5, p. 45). Deriving their rationale partly from mathematics or the use of numbers and ratios, these activities were used to provide an alternative means of accounting for natural and supernatural phenomena. There were indeed those who earned a living from their occult studies. Thus, astrology was widely practised, whilst alchemists were consulted for their secret knowledge of nature as well as for their professed powers of producing gold from base metals. Various forms of magic were practised, including geomancy, necromancy, natural magic, etc., whilst numerology, the study of the hidden powers of numbers, was widely considered a reputable mathematical pursuit. The underlying beliefs upon which these occult studies were founded included the following:

[margin notes: geomancy divination by means of a handful of earth thrown at random or by means of figures or lines

necromancy sorcery; witchcraft]

344 1 The Platonist idea that the universe was a living organism and, in particular, that the Earth itself and all its parts were sensitive, living and growing.

345 2 The idea that the universe as a whole was guided by laws which can be seen to be reflected in the behaviour of terrestrial things and, in particular, that there is a distinct correlation between phenomena in the heavens – the macrocosm – and the form and functions of the human body and its organs – the microcosm.

346 3 Astrological notions that there were unseen influences by which the heavenly bodies determined and preconditioned the course of events on Earth and in particular that the physical fortunes of human lives were positively and directly determined by the movements and conjunctions of the heavenly bodies.

347 4 Correspondences between the seven metals, the heavenly bodies and the days of the week:

Gold	Sun	Sunday
Silver	Moon	Monday
Iron	Mars	Tuesday (Anglo Saxon *Tiw*, Mars)
Quicksilver (Mercury)	Mercury	Wednesday (Fr. *mercredi*)
Tin	Jupiter	Thursday (Anglo Saxon *Thor*, Jupiter)
Copper	Venus	Friday (Fr. *vendredi*)
Lead	Saturn	Saturday

Such correlations were also extended to the principal organs of the body.

348   5   Animistic ideas, according to which any event, however spontaneous it appeared, was really caused by the activity of some personality or spirit.

You should not think of these as the important formative ideas of this period – Units 20–21 will give you a clear idea of the common beliefs of the vast majority of the people of Christendom. Nevertheless, they did find wide currency, forming the basis of superstition, popular astrology and occultism. They are an expression of the human desire to understand the unknown and to harness hidden powers both to foretell and if possible to control future events. You should bear all these ideas in mind in reading *The Alchemist*.

Neo-Platonism

[handwritten margin note: efficiency; potency; power to produce effect; virtue; force; energy; effectiveness.]

349   It is probably true to say that beliefs about the efficacy of occult powers derived support from the doctrines of Neo-Platonism, the last great school of Greek philosophy (see Unit 5, pp. 42–9).

The leading ideas of Neo-Platonism include a hierarchy of 'reality' expressed as a plurality of spheres of 'being' arranged in ascending order; the lowest sphere comprising all that is perceptible to the senses – all that exists in time and space. Each sphere derived its being from the one above and each derived being turned back to its superior in a movement of 'contemplative desire'. Each sphere was thus an image on a lower level of the one above and each individual reality was an image of a corresponding reality in the next higher sphere. But it was the return of the lower states which established each derived being in its own reality. The relationship between archetype and image runs clear through Neo-Platonic thought – a development of the Platonic doctrine of ideas (See Unit 5, pp. 39–40). Levels of being were also degrees of unity, for in each successively lower sphere the extent of Multiplicity, Separateness, Division and Limitation increased until atomic individualization in the space-time world was reached.

350   Light and number were regarded as closely related elements in the basic structure of the cosmos, for the latter was considered to be the self-unfolding of the light principle according to laws expressed in numbers. The laws of optics were thus regarded as fundamental to explanations in nature, whilst the Sun, as the source of light, occupied a central place in Neo-Platonic thought. Moreover, light was the agent through which the soul was able to work in the body and so the empirical and experimental science of physical optics was linked with beliefs about the spiritual world. The same light that informed the one illuminated the other.

The Late Medieval World Picture

AMENDMENTS TO ACADEMIC LISTS

Admitted			Left			
Jane Thrower	1D	F8	David Barr	2A	A3	
David Galbraith	3C	C2	Iain Ritchie	5A	F2	
Alistair Rutherford	2O	F4				

ABSENTEES - Tuesday, 25th April, 1978

1E   C.A.Cairney, J.Devine
1D   J.Kettrick, J.Kerr
1U   W.Henderson, C.Hughes, C.Shearer
1C   W.Armitage
1A   M.A.Teven
1T   S.Ferguson, E.Wood
1I   C.Dowell, D.Lang, K.Moore
1O   R.Reid
1N   W.Muir
1S   H.McKinnon

2E   M.Williams
2D   Nil
2U   R.Cramb, G.Russell
2C   J.Sloan
2A   Nil
2T   Nil
2I   W.Sharp
2O   A.Nicol
2N   A.Bett
2S   A.Armitage, A.Boon,   I.Symon

3E   Nil
3D   D.Gunn, N.Hamilton
3U   Nil

PART 4 A MEDIAEVAL/RENAISSANCE LITERARY PERSPECTIVE

by Brian Stone

A201 Course Supplement 1

CONTENTS

Introduction   97

Dramatic   97

Poetic   106

INTRODUCTION

400   Elizabethan literature bursts upon the reader new to it with the most extra-ordinary splendour. The plays, the poetic lyrics and narrative poetry, even the prose (vigorous and polysyllabic though it often is), seem modern in a way that most of the writing of even fifty years before does not; and much of the writing is better than anything that had preceded it in English, except that of Chaucer. Yet a fuller idea of Elizabethan literary achievement, and a better sense of what the Renaissance meant for England, can be developed if the reader has some acquaintance with the writing and thinking of the previous age. In those parts of the existing correspondence material ahead, which are intended as an introduction to your Elizabethan literary and dramatic studies, you will find a few minutes' work on Chaucer, a brief account of mediaeval drama, the study of one short, early sixteenth-century religious play, and some extended work on allegory. In this unit we want to improve the balance – and to widen the scope slightly, as well as further integrating literary matters with other elements of the course.

401   Accordingly, I shall now offer some mediaeval and other background to the Elizabethan drama, briefly illuminating dramatic and related arts before the Tudor period began and referring to their place in society. I shall also offer brief comparative textual study of mediaeval and Elizabethan lyric poetry, together with further information about courtly love and its place in literature, and a little about poetry in general. The scope of the work will be mainly north-west European, except when study of an English text narrows and concentrates the focus.

1   DRAMATIC (mainly about popular activities)

402   I want in this short section to give some sort of mediaeval background against which you may place your subsequent study of the performing arts during the Renaissance. By 'performing arts' I do not mean just plays, though the mediaeval religious drama, with its associated ceremonies, is the most important single development of which to take account. I have in mind the processions, tournaments, pageants, triumphs and masques organized by royalty and nobility; the activities of the various kinds of entertainers, both itinerant ones and those who were retainers of the great – poets, minstrels, mimes and jesters. I am thinking of the interrelation of these, and of their continuous evolution towards the state of affairs we recognize as Elizabethan. In the late sixteenth century we shall find that:

403   a   Troupes of professional actors existed, under the protection of royalty and nobility and generally under attack by civic authority and the new reformed churches.

404   b   Tournaments had virtually ceased, but processions, pageants, triumphs and masques still flourished as political shows, scripted, designed and even directed by professional dramatists and artists.

405   c   The religious drama, especially in England, had declined under Government disapproval, and some of its elements had passed into the professional secular theatre.

406   d   As society evolved from feudal to mercantile and early capitalistic, an

economy dominated by country became one in which the city was steadily increasing in importance.

407   e   As this change in society proceeded, and a cultured middle class developed, the milieux in which the performing arts and literature were experienced also changed. Poems circulated in manuscript, without being composed primarily for singing or recitation at gatherings; and stories were printed in books (which of course followed the invention of printing and the consequent spread of literacy) rather than chanted or recited in noble halls and public places. In music, instrumental compositions began to appear, and with the same impetus of printing they were disseminated more widely, as musical literacy and hence formal musical accomplishment spread. Naturally the old practices continued while the new ones evolved. From about the end of the fifteenth century, the proportion of secular works of art increased rapidly.

408   All the arts reflected that widening and changed consciousness that we associate with the idea of 'the Renaissance'. In that consciousness, some of the elements which you will come across and discuss on this course – and you should already be aware of the danger of taking such marks of periodization for gospel – are:

a loosening of the hold of the sacred perspective on minds;

God dominates as before, but Man thinks he disposes as well as proposes;

the dominance of the European perspective diminishes, as the national perspectives become more important.

409   Classical works of art, literature and thought increasingly come to bear on sixteenth-century culture through secular rather than priestly meditation: the Renaissance makes its own use of antiquity, going beyond the devotional wish to find moral examples and instruction there, and seeking the deeper and more varied meanings and impulses connected with sensuous, individual, passionate life, with freer speculation in the world of ideas, and with concepts of social life and personal morality not necessarily associated with the Christian system. Of course, even in the high Middle Ages, there had been speculative thought based on reason, as the work of Roger Bacon and Nicholas of Cusa (whom you will meet in Unit 15) shows; and in the high Renaissance there was – as the reception of Copernicus' discoveries concerning the structure of the universe was to show – to be just the same kind of appeal to the Scriptures and the established teaching of the Church when new ideas and discoveries were published, as in the Middle Ages.

410   We must also consider, besides works of literary and dramatic art, their musical and other implications, the activities of ordinary people at times of celebration and relaxation. In doing this, we must think about the nature of the expressive arts themselves, and why we concern ourselves with them on this course. In primitive societies, dancing, singing and various mimetic activities were organic to the detail of lived life, and social routine and religious ceremonies included them as a matter of course; but in modern society, especially of the European type, such activities are no longer organic to the customs and rhythms of private and public life, though of course alternatives and surrogates of them exist here and there. Whatever the many reasons for this change, the sad observable fact is that human beings' natural demonstrative and expressive faculties have withered, and the arts through which they once functioned, where they survive, figure mostly in the repertory of professionals. We must ask ourselves of the performing arts especially, but also of all the arts, why they existed in the forms we know about during the period we are studying, what needs they satisfied, and why they were always such bones of contention in religious and political circles. I put these questions speculatively, and shall not

try to answer any of them, though I shall discuss religious and, to some extent, political, attitudes towards the performing arts.

411 The intention is not to survey this enormous field, but to highlight activities and attitudes relevant to the study of Renaissance performing arts, and of Elizabethan drama in particular.

412 Two gentle warnings for a start. The first is: do not expect to consider dramatic matters separately: discussion of performing activities will often involve music and the visual arts, and almost always involves discussion of matters religious, political and social. And the second warning is: develop a different attitude towards the recorded history of the performing arts from the one you normally take towards that of literature, music and art. This is because the record of performance is both thin and unsatisfactory. We can see and touch actual mediaeval stained glass, or look at a (probably retouched or restored) mediaeval painting; we can (although differences in interpretation are wider than in interpreting music of later periods) play mediaeval music; we can supplement (with speculation about mediaeval rhetoric and guild organization) the meagre records, mainly from account lists, of how mediaeval plays were staged; and we can read mediaeval literature. But we cannot see a mediaeval play in performance, or watch and hear a minstrel rendering a romance or fabliau, or a mime in a market place holding up the local gentry to ridicule, and we cannot watch villagers dancing in graveyards on their days off (a common cause of complaint by bishops). All we can do is to read what observers, usually but not always hostile, said about such activities. It is hard to counter the clerical bias of mediaeval records and literature generally; but I shall try not to speculate too wildly.

413 In this brief essay I shall be concerned with attitudes and activities, and their survival into our study period. It may seem illogical to consider attitudes before the activities which give rise to the attitudes, but since the latter were expressed in writing which has survived for us to read – sermons, records, criticism and the changing law itself – they constitute a kind of constant yardstick by which we can measure what was happening, even if we cannot be exact about the happening itself: the dance, the mime, the recitation, the performed play.

414 A conventional mediaeval view of public performers, which has the useful merit, for us, of also being in part descriptive, is that of Thomas de Chabham, the Sub-dean of Salisbury, who wrote in a Penitential early in the fourteenth century:

> There are three sorts of actor. Some transform and transfigure themselves with shameful dance and gesture, either indecently unclothing themselves, or putting on loathsome masks, and all such are to be condemned, unless they give up their practice. In addition there are others who do nothing in particular but act slanderously, having no proper home, but frequent the courts of the great and utter taunting scandals about people who are absent, in order to please the rest. These also are to be condemned. . . Besides these, there is a third kind of actors who have musical instruments for delighting men, and of these there are two sorts. Some haunt public drinking-places and lascivious gatherings, where they sing gossipy songs to persuade people to wantonness, and such are to be condemned like the others. Besides these there are others called jongleurs, who sing stories of princes and lives of the saints, and solace men in their sickness or trouble, and do not commit numberless indecencies as do the men and women dancers and others who work on corrupt imaginations. . . If they do not do these (latter) things, but sing with accompanying instruments stories of princes and other subjects which may bring solace to men, as was said above, such may well be given sustenance, as Pope Alexander said.
>
> (Translated by BS from E. K. Chambers (1903) *The Medieval Stage*, vol. II, Appendix G, pp. 262–3, Oxford University Press.)

415   The historic position of the Church on acting goes back to Judaic teaching against assuming disguise, and against image-making, an activity clearly cognate with the representation by one person of other characters; and to the bad experience of the early Christians at the hands of the entertainers of the Roman Empire. Throughout the long period after the decay of what may be called 'legitimate theatre' at the hands of Imperial censorship, public performers in Rome had functioned predominantly in light vein – bawdy, satire, lewd and even naked dancing, and rough knockabout farce; and while it was fashionable and acceptable to do so, they naturally made fun of the new religion of Christianity, and did their turns at shows during which Christians were killed, either ceremonially, or in unequal combat with men or animals 'to make a Roman holiday.' So the Christian position on public entertainers – and please remember that the concept of a professionally trained actor who would perform in a serious play with a 'literary' text does not develop until we are almost into the Renaissance proper – was early established by men like Tertullian (c.160–c.225) and St John Chrysostom (c.350–407). Here is Tertullian pointing out to a non-Christian audience how the mimes bring even pagan religion into disrepute:

416   The rest of your licentious wits also work for your pleasure through the shame of your gods. Look at the farces of the Lentuluses and Hostiliuses and consider whether you are laughing at the jokes and tricks of the mimes or at your gods. Themes like Anubis as a lover . . . , a man-Moon . . . , a tormented Diana . . . the last testament of dead Jove, and three hungry Herculeses are treated ridiculously. The art of these writers is always employed on this kind of filth. The sun-god (Sol) mourns over his son, who has been cast from heaven, and you laugh; Cybele sighs for her disdainful shepherd and you do not blush. . . . A mask representing your god is worn by a base and notorious fellow; an impure body trained to this art by emasculation represents a Minerva or a Hercules – do you not think that their majesty is outraged and their divinity prostituted in the midst of your applause?

        (*Apologeticus*, xv, quoted by Allardyce Nicoll (1963) *Mimes, Masks and Miracles*, Cooper Square, N.Y., p. 113.)

417   And here is St John Chrysostom, writing of Christian Byzantium, concentrating with scorn on the appearance, training and morality of the profession:

        What tumult! What satanic clamour! What diabolic dress! Here comes a youth, with hair combed back, who makes himself effeminate in look, in manner, in dress – aye, in everything takes on the shape and guise of a tender girl. Here comes an old man with his hair all shaved, who has cast off shame with his hair, and who stands there to receive slaps on the face and who is prepared for all that is said and done. And the women too! With uncovered heads, all shame lost, they stand talking to the people, aiming at unchastity, arousing the minds of the spectators to wantonness and obscenity. For these wanton words, these ridiculous manners, these foolish tonsures, these ways of walking, these dresses, these voices, that softness of limbs, that winking of the eyes, these pipes and flutes, these dramas and arguments – aye, all are full of utter wantonness. Here are to be seen naught but fornication, adultery, courtesan women, men pretending to be women, and soft-limbed boys.

        (*Hom VI*;. in *Matt. xxxvii* and *xxxviii*, quoted by Nicoll, *op. cit.*, p. 138.)

418   The comedian with his hair shaved off is common in mediaeval illustrations, and of course with his false bald head he is still familiar to us today, as a circus clown or professional mime. The comic ploy of face-slapping survives too.

    In a passage which is most instructive of the interaction between drama and ritual, Chrysostom attacks the Arians (a heretical fourth century Christian sect which denied the consubstantiality of the Son with the Father) for their sensuous style of worship:

They show themselves no better than madmen, agitating and moving their bodies, uttering strange sounds, engaging in customs foreign to the things of the Spirit. They introduce the habits of mimes and dancers into sacred places. Their minds are darkened by what they have heard and seen in the theatres. They confuse theatrical action with the ceremonies of the Church.

(cf Reich, i, 135, quoted by Nicoll, *op. cit.*, p. 139.)

But mimes had their defenders. Allardyce Nicoll (*op. cit.*, p. 132) cites Roman opinions of them: 'The most loquacious hands, the speaking fingers, the clamorous silence' and 'A marvellous art it is which makes the limbs speak when the tongue is silent.'

419   St Augustine admitted their power over him in his errant youth: 'The scenic spectacles enraptured me. In my time I had a violent passion for these spectacles which were full of the images of my miseries and of the amorous flames of fire which devoured me.' (*Confessions*, iii, 2–3, quoted by Nicoll, *op. cit.* p. 140.)

420   The kindlier point of view is expressed rarely. Choricius (sixth century) defends the mimes with an argument exactly like the one with which Elizabethans later defended their theatre against Puritan attacks:

> Of what indeed can the mimes be accused – unless you charge them with the crime of not imitating the better only? And how could they be worthy of the name 'mime', which is theirs because of their portrayal of life, if they were to delineate some parts of life and to neglect others? . . . Instead of blaming the mimes, blame those who do commit the evil actions which are themselves the basis of the miming, or imitation of evil. When we thus reflect on the matter we see that actors are not guilty of any crime.

(Quoted by Nicoll, *op. cit.*, p. 142, from Reich, i, 204–22.)

421   But Church hostility to acting and associated performing arts, thus firmly established, remained constant throughout our period.[1] And it was left to lay people of all ranks to delight themselves on the whole without specific blessing. Henry V had fifteen minstrels on his payroll for his Agincourt campaign (1415), and there are many records of minstrels, jugglers, acrobats and so forth congregating at religious feasts, formal courts, tournaments and fairs.

422   One significant thing to bear in mind in this skimming over a wide scene, is a development which appears to have occurred only in northern Europe. Whenever there was a *troupe* of entertainers, whether employed by a great person or self-employed and itinerant, very often the member with the best standing and most pay was the *poet*. Historians of the theatre tend to think this was because the Roman mimes and the inheritors of their tradition, when they moved northwards, met the Germanic poets, the *scops*, and the bards of the Celtic civilization, who were the poets and chanters of the sagas and myths of the northern tribes. The resultant fusion of the two traditions added weight and dignity to a varied profession which in the south, after the decay of the 'true' theatre, had depended mostly on scurrility, bawdy and the popular generally. It was in Italy during the sixteenth century that the recognizably Roman comic tradition produced the Commedia dell'Arte, a school of comic acting depending on stock characters and situations which has integrally influenced comic dramaturgy and acting from Molière to Pirandello and after. Molière – in the late seventeenth century! – was denied burial in holy ground on account of his profession, but the descendant of the lofty *scop* could be offered priestly hospitality in the high Middle Ages – as the above quotation from Thomas de Chabham shows.

423   I have just drawn together four elements of my theme: the decay of the Roman theatre, the continued preference of the educated for a performing art based on

[1] For the different and changing attitude of the Catholic and other Churches towards *religious* drama, see paras. 425 and 430–33.

speech and writing about lofty subjects, the ubiquity and vigour of popular expressive idioms, and orthodox attitudes to all of these. Since the art of the theatre had been virtually dead since the triumph of Christianity in the late Roman Empire, I wonder what the attitude of Thomas de Chabham would have been had he been able to see Terence's plays (or those of any other Latin dramatist of standing) as they were actually performed? Since the tenth-century canoness Hroswitha, who called herself 'the strong voice of Gandersheim', while admiring the style, condemned the 'shameless' material of Terence's plays and wrote six 'Terentian' comedies transforming his themes so that in her plays the virgin life is praised, it is to be doubted whether Thomas would have extended his approval to Terence. And to judge by the illustrations to ninth-century codices of Terence's work, which show the poet reading his text, while masked mimes perform the action, (see Nicoll, *op cit.*, figures 102–3, pp. 54–5) some mediaeval people must have had little idea how a classical play had been performed. *(← codex 'a book')*

424 What appeared real and acceptable to the official guardians of culture then, as indeed it does to our own guardians of culture – the educationalists, the professions and government, the religious, the philosophers and so forth – were words which could be written down, read silently and thought about, or spoken aloud.

Words are counters which can be more or less pinned down to identifiable meanings, and so invite their users to compose structures of reasoning and logical sequence, but when they are accompanied or replaced by what may be dangerously sensuous, alarmingly explicit yet infinitely suggestive movements of the body, such as belong to the arts of mime, acting and dancing, the resultant performance tends to defy attempts to incorporate its meaning and value in a moral educational system.

425 But so far I have been writing of performing arts which in the main have nothing to do with religion. When we turn to the 'respectable' performing arts, we find that drama is one with all the other arts in the thinking of the mediaeval Church. The poetry and music of the latter, the architecture and decoration of its cathedrals and churches, showed that the Church well-understood the diverse manifestations of the performing arts, and permitted them, provided that they did not operate against religion. This is not the place to go into the origins of mediaeval religious drama – I personally do not believe that it 'originated', but rather that the impulse of mimesis is fundamental to all peoples, so that it always existed, even within an organization which was as hostile to secular performance as we have seen the early and mediaeval Church to have been. Suffice it to say that from the eleventh to the sixteenth century in England there was religious drama of different kinds: whether it took place as part of the service, or in connection with religious feasts or processions, whether it was based on biblical or non-biblical material, whether it was in Latin, or Norman–French, or the vernacular English, whether it took place within or outside the Church, it was always under the control, and often the direction too, of senior ecclesiastics, who regarded it as the natural and fruitful activity of a Christian society.

426 So it is appropriate to distinguish between two main kinds of acting, the one first discussed, and the one now mooted, which was the proper means of representing sacred or near-sacred subjects. On the whole, this latter took its gestures from the law court and the pulpit; it seems, from the plentiful narrative painting from the Middle Ages which survives, that a range of stiff gestures, approximating to a didactic sign language, was used. You can get a good idea of these from Bertram Joseph's little book, *Elizabethan Acting* (Oxford University Press 1951), in which illustrations from Elizabethan manuals of

mimicry; the copying by an animal, as protective measure of the colour of its environment or of the characteristics of another animal

rhetoric figure instructively. The language of this kind of drama came from common speech, from the Bible and devotional writing, and its verse structures from the inherited culture – the Anglo-Saxon alliterative line and style crossed by dominating Romance metres. But both the traditions of performance briefly mentioned here helped to mould the style of Elizabethan acting and indeed play-writing, as we find them discussed in Hamlet's first scene with the players (2.ii).

alliteration beginning of two or more words in close succession with same sound.

427   I should like to turn now to dance, the 'first art', which in its primary form is the bodily expression of ecstasy and magical power. Dance, the unconscious and social art until, individualized, it becomes conscious (I incorporate there two phrases of Cecil Sharp's, which I believe are in his *The Dance* (Halton and Truscott Smith, 1924)). Dance, which in its aristocratically evolved form Plato commended 'for the acquisition of noble, harmonious and graceful attitudes' (A. H. Franks (1965) *Social Dance*, Routledge and Kegan Paul). Dance, which in its popular forms the mediaeval Church regarded as the art especially appropriate to the Devil. I mentioned dancing in churchyards: probably, the church being the natural focal point for community activity, old social rites of celebration of mixed and partly pagan origin took place there. The Elizabethan puritan, Stubbs, particularly condemned May-games, in which a maypole, ancient phallic symbol, was erected and danced round.

428   From time to time I have referred to dance as if it was always included in priestly denunciation. Not so. We must distinguish between various kinds of dancing, especially when we are studying a period at the height of which, following Plato, noble and harmonious dancing, being man's best earthly imitation of God's perfection in controlling the motion of the spheres, was a gentleman's necessary accomplishment. (Remember this when you watch television programme number 6 and when you come to study Davies' poem 'Orchestra' *The Penguin Book of Elizabethan Verse*, pp. 85–90.) More than this, dancing was seen as a natural culmination of rejoicing at pageants, triumphs and masques. First the professionals danced, and then the whole gathering. Sometimes royalty and nobility danced separately from the rest but at the same time. Sometimes they joined with the professionals, and sometimes the whole company mingled in the dance. This was a reflection of a tradition which I believe goes as far back as recorded history.

429   Long before the gentlemanly dance for grace and health, which may be exemplified by Socrates' learning new dances from Aspasia at the age of sixty ('Am I to be blamed for reducing the corpulence of my body by a little dancing?' – Lincoln Kirstein (1935) *Dance*, Dance Horizons, p. 39), there was religious ritual dance. Akhnaton, the royal proselytizer of a new religion in Egypt in the fourteenth century BC, almost certainly danced in worship of his new god, the sun disc. But the history of the dance is not our concern at the moment. What is, is that dancing has often been an element in Christian worship, no doubt legitimized by the well-known biblical reference to King David dancing 'before the Lord' (II Samuel 6, 14). Lincoln Kirstein (*op. cit.*, pp. 61–3) quotes a passage from a Gnostic romance known as the Acts of John, in which, at the end of the Last Supper, Jesus leads the disciples in a ring-dance – the established form of holy dances which aim symbolically to imitate the harmony of heaven. (Possibly the writer of the Acts of John was aware that the event he described was in tune with Platonic theory about the harmony of the spheres.) Jesus, exhorting his disciples, significantly says: 'Those who do not dance will not comprehend what shall befall'. Unsanctified holy writing that, but adequately sanctified are the dancings (usually clockwise ring dances), during church services recorded throughout the mediaeval and Renaissance period. They survived as late as the nineteenth century in one or two places, Seville Cathedral being one. But all the same, ballet dancers in the Milan

proselyte convert.

opera could not attend mass until well into the present century. Their dancing may have been considered the wrong kind – possibly because a ballet company was regarded by bloods young and old as an appropriate assembly from which to cull their mistresses? At any rate, they could not have danced as angels do: St Basil (c.330–79) had recommended the 'faithful to practise dancing as much as possible upon earth, since it was the principal occupation of angels in heaven' (Kirstein, *op. cit.*, p. 92). Such shows of spiritual and even mystical sensuousness came, during the Reformation, to suffer Protestant condemnation, together with the use of images, incense and the rest. But moderate Protestants like Luther and Melanchthon approved of the dance on humanist grounds.

430   It remains, in this section tracing performance activities and attitudes towards them in the Middle Ages, to say a word or two about the change which took place with the arrival in the sixteenth century of Protestant Christianity, with its own ideas and their impact on the developing English theatre. As we have seen, the mediaeval Church tested different kinds of acting, singing and dancing by their bearing on the virtuous life and religion. Priestly discouragement of the arts and pleasures generally was by no means uniform, and among numerous examples of a catholicity of attitude, I should like to mention the Franciscan acceptance of, even delight in, joyous human activities which, according to St Francis and his followers, helped to justify an optimistic outlook on life. The Church did not disapprove of anything in the field of the arts merely because it gave pleasure or relaxation from serious matters, although some of its zealots did so. But a characteristically Puritan attitude did, during the sixteenth century in England, combine with Government hostility to anything directly associated with Rome to get rid of the religious drama. The original political act of hostility towards Rome, the assertion of religious supremacy within his own dominions by Henry VIII by 1534 (for the detail, see Units 24–5, pp. 62–4 and especially para. 34.3.2. on p. 64), had little to do with a genuinely Protestant theology, but did provide the political framework, within which, during the reign of Edward VI (1547–53) and after the Catholic reign of Mary, with the return to England of Protestant exiles from Europe and especially Switzerland, that theology could flourish. That first action of Henry VIII's began the anti-artistic movement which culminated, in the English Revolution of the mid-seventeenth century, in the removal of images, sculptures and paintings from places of worship, the closing of the theatres, and a concentration on plainness which extended even to styles of speech and dress.

431   Let us see how Calvin's Consistory, as an example of Protestant theory working in practice, censured pleasures. This is how Williston Walker, a sympathetic historian, puts it:

> No age or distinction exempted one from its censures. Men and women were examined as to their religious knowledge, their criticisms of ministers, their absence from sermons, their use of charms, their family quarrels, as well as to more serious offences. Other examples, from the later activity of the Consistory in Calvin's time, show disciplinary procedure ... for having fortunes told by gipsies, against a goldsmith for making a chalice; ... for dancing; for possessing a copy of the Golden Legend,[1] ... having a copy of Amadis de Gaules,[2] or singing a song defamatory of Calvin.
>
> (*John Calvin the Organizer of Reformed Protestantism*, London, 1906, pp. 304 ff., quoted in your set book – François Wendel (1969) *Calvin*, Fontana, 3rd Impression.)

432   The basis upon which Calvin and his followers approved such censoriousness is to be found in Calvin's *Institutes*, in which the concept of divine righteousness operates in such a way as to sanction the most rigorous repression of the arts, among other activities:

[1] Popular collection of saints' lives, homilies, and other devotional (Catholic) writing.
[2] A collection of romances about a Spanish hero.

For whoever beholds God in all his works easily turns his mind away from all vain cogitations. That is the denial of ourselves which Christ so earnestly demands of all his disciples for their first apprenticeship: and by which, when once it occupies the heart of man, first vanity, pride and ostentation are exterminated; and then avarice, intemperance, superfluity and all revelling, with the other vices that are born of love of ourselves.

(Calvin's *Institutes* III, 7, 2, quoted by Wendel, *op. cit.*, p. 248.)

433 With such a blanket condemnation of pleasure, it is no wonder that Calvin's approval of the *religious* drama, for all practical purposes, was submerged by the tide of zealot reform. And it is no wonder that among the hated figures of Elizabethan and Jacobean comedy, the Puritan (there are two in *The Alchemist*, and you may be familiar with Shakespeare's Malvolio in *Twelfth Night*) is most prominently exploited and ridiculed. The curious thing about the European religious drama at this time is that, even within Catholic communities, it begins to wither. Perhaps, when Catholics felt themselves to be under attack for encouraging spectacular entertainment as part of their religious practice, they might very well have examined what they did with a view to either meeting or blunting the criticism. Thus we find, as early as 1576, French and Italian bishops prohibiting dramatic processions and plays in their dioceses. An additional reason for the decline was the ruinous expense of the competitive mounting of such spectacular and long-lasting shows, which interrupted and impoverished routine commercial life. Clearly a European movement against religious drama had set in, even in countries where Protestant elements did not wield direct political power. Yet the Jesuits, who were prominent in the Counter-Reformation, used drama in their schools for its educational value.

434 Concerning aspects of the mediaeval religious drama proper, which are relevant to the study of Elizabethan drama, I have only two points to make, of which you should take account when reading Cicely Havely's introduction (Unit 31, pp. 5–10).

436 The first point is that *all* the elements of performance mentioned in this essay, including the various creative acts of predetermining the nature and scope of performances – telling the tale, specifying the music, the dance, the action – went into the religious drama. The latter subject is sometimes taught as if the only important thing about its origin is that it developed step by step from the drama inherent but not manifest in the Mass. But, as Richard Axton makes clear in *European Drama of the Early Middle Ages* (Hutchinson 1974), substantial and artistically-written secular plays, as well as partly religious plays written in popular idiom in the vernacular, were performed in quite early times. Those sophisticated dramatic artefacts, the English Cycle plays, which in the form we have them derive mostly from the fifteenth century, embody diverse literary, musical and acting traditions. A similar point could be made with even more force in the field of lyric (i.e. usually sung) poetry. Religious lyrics often had themes and music derived from secular lyrics, as the many charming songs addressed to the Virgin Mary, and written in the style of the courtly love lyric, testify. In all artistic, as in most other matters, developments in mediaeval England were either closely related to, or followed, developments in northern France.

The second point concerns the impact of the classical drama on the Elizabethan tradition, to which only passing reference is made in your study material. Schoolroom-orientated classicism would have had Elizabethan dramatists writing in the style of Seneca and Terence. But the living and diverse traditions to which I have referred permeated the world of performance and entertainment so thoroughly that the Elizabethan public would not stomach an antiquarian theatre of pure Roman rhetoric, although naturally the universities could and did. Senecan plays were indeed written, but unless they contained diversity of action and mode in the popular and accepted style, they failed. A characteristic of the development period, when the so-called Tudor interludes were being written and performed, is the effort of scholarly dramatists like Henry Medwall (f.l. 1486) and John Heywood (?1497–?1580) to be at once faithful to their classical masters and in tune with pragmatic English dramatic convention.

2   POETIC (mainly about courtly love)

437   Since one common basis for both mediaeval and Renaissance love poetry, narrative as well as lyric, is the system of ideas that we call 'courtly love', and since the main secular subject of the lyric throughout the period was love, we must at least develop a working notion of what this 'courtly love' was.

438   I remember watching, many years ago, a television quiz programme of some sort in which two of the participants were A. J. Ayer the philosopher and Eartha Kitt, the American singer. The subject under examination was love; and Professor Ayer suddenly observed that love as we know it was invented in the south of France in the twelfth century – or something like that. And Eartha Kitt's eyes rounded hugely in comic incredulity. What Professor Ayer meant by that, I believe, was that our cultural and in some senses our actual attitude towards, and expectations of, love derive from the ideas of courtly love expressed in the lyric poetry written in the early Middle Ages in the langue d'oc, the Romance vernacular of Provence, which one can still hear spoken in the south of France and Aquitaine. C. M. Bowra (*Mediaeval Love-Song*, the John Coffin Memorial Lecture, 1961, the Athlone Press, ULP, p. 8) echoes Ayer:

> Courtly love, as this poetry embodies it, is a most unusual invention of the human spirit, and for some two hundred years the love-songs of western Europe were dominated by it.

439   The courtly lover falls in love with his lady at first sight, finding her perfect in every quality. He abases himself before her, and vows her eternal service. This service that he gives her, he regards as a sacred duty; in maintaining it, he exercises all knightly virtues, such as bravery, chivalry, magnanimity, modesty, gentleness and good faith. And so doing, he establishes his eligibility to her favours, but no rights to obtain them; however faithful and virtuous his service, he remains absolute in his submission to her will. In fact, the greater his submissiveness, the greater his virtue. From all this it followed that love was regarded as the noblest activity of man, and thus it was more than a constant aim, it was positively a duty, to be in love.

440   C. S. Lewis provocatively observed:

> It seems—or it seemed to us till lately—a natural thing that love (under certain conditions) should be regarded as a noble and ennobling passion: it is only if we imagine ourselves trying to explain this doctrine to Aristotle, Virgil, St Paul, or the author of *Beowulf*, that we become aware how far from natural it is. Even our code of etiquette, with its rule that women always have precedence, is a legacy from courtly love, and is felt to be far from natural in modern Japan or India. Many of the features of this sentiment, as it was known to the Troubadours, have indeed disappeared; but this must not blind us to the fact that the most momentous and the most revolutionary elements in it have made the background of European literature for eight hundred years. French poets . . .

effected a change which has left no corner of our ethics, our imagination or our daily life untouched, and they erected impassable barriers between us and the classical past or the Oriental present. Compared with this revolution the Renaissance is a mere ripple on the surface of literature.

(*The Allegory of Love*, Oxford 1936, 1953 edition, pp. 3–4.)

441   The whole notion of courtly love, by its insistence on the twin bases of chivalry and service, reveals its aristocratic provenance. It belongs to a feudal world in which the good things of life, among them passionate idealistic love, are available only to those of high birth, and more particularly to those of high birth whose manners and behaviour are similarly elevated. But although the spirit of this kind of adoration seems religious, courtly love was in fundamental conflict with Christianity, because it not only allowed but exalted the act of physical love, which it represented, usually outside the marriage bond, as the means of ultimate spiritual fulfilment. The quasi-religious spirit of courtly love largely depended on characteristics found in extra-marital relationship. 'Inborn suffering', its key feature, was compounded of such elements as excessive desire, separation, clandestine operation and deprivation.

442   The contemporary work which gives an account (rather a wry one, incidentally) of courtly love (a term, by the way, which was first used in 1883 to translate the description 'amour courtois' given to courtly love by the mediaevalist Gaston Paris) is *De Arte Honeste Amandi* by Andreas Capellanus, who was chaplain to the Countess of Champagne, daughter of the famous Eleanor of Aquitaine. (Eleanor, wife first to Louis VII of France and then to the cultured King Henry II of England, was a famous patroness of the arts and president of courts of love.) An easily available translated and abridged version is F. W. Locke (ed.) (1957) *The Art of Courtly Love*, Ungar, New York. Andreas's little treatise, much of which is in dialogue form, represents northern developments of courtly love, among which one may note some major differences from the original Provençal ideal. Andreas stresses the ideal of mutual love, makes much more of the desirability of physical consummation and rather less of the man's selfless adoration of his love-object, and takes a consistently moral line about the behaviour of lovers.

443   Then, since he is a priest ('Capellanus' means 'chaplain') he rounds off his work with a section entitled 'The Rejection of Love', in which he advances a conventional argument, based on the scriptures and the teaching of the mediaeval Church, in favour of the chaste life and the marriage bond. He even includes the usual savage denigration of women: 'A woman's desire is to get rich through love . . . Woman is also a miser . . . envious . . . a slanderer . . . a slave to her belly.' Of course it was all the fault of Eve, 'who although she was created by the hand of God without man's agency was not afraid to eat the forbidden fruit and for her gluttony was deservedly driven from her home in Paradise'. (F. W. Locke, *op. cit.*, pp. 48–9.)

444   Pause to consider to what extent the system outlined by Andreas might reasonably be called an 'invention'. You may think it hard to do this without any real idea of how 'love' was treated in earlier literatures; but I cannot give that kind of broad survey with any sort of conviction. But if you have any reading background, try to remember how love is treated in, say, the Old Testament or the Odyssey, and compare those treatments, and that of Andreas, with your own ideas of what love between man and woman is in reality.

445   My guess is that, since love is so various, you found some aspects of courtly love that accorded with your view of love in our real world, but that there are other

aspects (such as the obsession with class and formal manners) of it which strike you as artificial. It was a thirteenth-century Paris poet, Rutebeuf, author of plays, lyrics and religious poetry, who said, 'Love is only for the rich!'

446   Without more ado then, please read the following four poems, with their brief introductory notes, in something of a comparative spirit, noting similarities and dissimilarities of form and content.

447   The first is by Guillaume de Poitiers (1071–1127), the first Troubadour. He was Duke of Aquitaine and ruler of the biggest domain in France; he organized the First Crusade (1101–2), and was a military and amatory adventurer who several times fell foul of the Church. Here is perhaps his best-known stanza, the first of a poem probably written before his departure on pilgrimage to Compostella after the lifting of an excommunication in 1117:

> Pos de chantar m'es pres talentz,
> Farai un vers don sui dolenz
> Mai no serai obedienz
> En Peitau ni en Lemozi.

> Since I long to sing
> I will make a verse which saddens me
> Nevermore shall I be a servant (of love)
> In Poitou or in Limousin.

448   The whole poem by Guillaume that we shall consider is a spring song; and I print the original not because I expect you to know the langue d'oc, but because even if you have no smattering of French and Latin, it is possible to get some sense and music from the poem by reading it aloud, provided you have the literal translation at hand.

449

> Ab la dolcor del temps nòvel
> Folhon li bòsc, a li aucèl
> Chanton chascús en lor latí
> Segon lo vèrs del nòvel chan;
> Adonc està ben qu'òm s'aisí
> D'aissò don òm a plus talan.

> In the sweetness of the new spring
> the woods blossom and the birds sing
> each in its own tongue
> in the rhythm of a new song;
> Now it is right that every man
> Should delight his heart in what he
>   most desires.

> De lai don plus m'es bon e bèl
> Non vei messagèr ni sagel,
> Per que mos còrs non dòrm ni ri,
> Ni mo m'aus traire adenan,
> Tro que sacha ben de la fi
> S'el' es aissí com eu deman.

> From where she is, good to me and
>   lovely,
> Comes neither messenger nor sealed
>   letter
> So my heart neither sleeps nor laughs,
> Nor dare I take a step further
> Till I know whether she will be in
> agreement with me as I desire.

> La nòstr' amor vai enaissi
> Com la branca de l'albespí
> Qu'està sobre l'arbre en treman,
> La nuòit, a la plòja ez al gèl,
> Tro l'endeman, que'l sols s'espan
> Per las fuèlhas vertz e'l ramèl.

> Our love proceeds
> like a spray of hawthorn
> which trembles on the tree
> at night, exposed to rain and frost,
> until the next day, the sun shines
>   through
> the green leaves and branches.

> Enquèr me membra d'un matí
> Que nos fezem de guerra fi,
> E que'm donèt un don tan gran,
> Sa drudari e son anèl:
> Enquèr me lais Dièus viure tan
> Qu'aja mas mans sotz son mantèl!

> I still remember the morning
> we ended all our conflict,
> and she made me such a great gift,
> all her love, and her ring:
> May God let me live long enough
> To have my hands (again) under her
>   gown.

Qu'eu non ai sonh d'estranh latí   For I don't heed strange talk
Qu'm parta de mon Bon Vezí,   Which might separate me from my
Qu'eu sai de paraulas com van   Beautiful Neighbour;
Ab un brèu sermon que s'espèl,   I know how words are taken
Que tal se van d'amor gaban,   And how brief speech can be diffused
Nos n'avem la pèssa e'l coutèl.   in rumour.
                                        Such people can brag of their love,
                                        While we have the portion and the
                                          knife (to cut it).

(Original text from Pierre Bec (ed): *Nouvelle Anthologie de la lyrique occitane du moyen age*, 2nd ed. Aubanel, pp. 175–6.

450   The second poem is an anonymous English one from MS. Harley 2253, the lucky survival of which has given us the most distinguished courtly love and religious lyrics of the early fourteenth century. Since the manuscript is thought to have been written about 1320, some of the poems may be much older. In any case, the courtly love tradition had been established long enough to have hardened: yet the freshness breaks through.

451   Bytwene Mersh and Averil
        When spray biginneth to springe,
    The lutel foul hath her will   little bird
        On hyrè lude to synge.   voice
        Ich libbè in lovè-longinge   live
        For semlokest of allè thyng;   most beautiful
        He may be blisse bringe;   he=she
          Icham in her bandoun.   I am in her power

        An hendy hap ichabbe yhent,   I have received good fortune
        Ichot from hevene it is me sent;   I know
        From alle wymmen mi love is lent,   taken away
          Ant lyht on Alysoun.   has settled

    On heu hire her is fayr ynoh,   in colour her hair
        Hire browè broune, hire eye blake;
    With lossom chere he on me loh,   lovely face she looked on me
        With middel smal ant wel ymake.   waist small and shapely
        Bote he me wolle to hirè take   unless she
        Fortè buen hire owen make   to be her own mate
        Longè to lyven ichulle forsake   I shall not live long
          Ant feye fallen adoun.   doomed
            An hendy hap, etc.

    Nihtes when y wende ant wake,   at night, turn
        Forthi myn wongès waxeth won;   therefore my cheeks grow pale
    Leuedi, al for thinè sake   lady
        Longinge is ylent me on.   has come upon me
        In world nis non so wyter mon   nowhere is there a man so wise
        That al hire bounte tellè con;   that can recount all her excellence

    Hire swyre is whittore then the swon,   neck, whiter
        Ant feyrest may in toune.   fairest girl living
          An hendy hap, etc.

    Icham for wowyng al forwake,   I am worn out with lying awake
                                               for love

    Wery so water in wore,   As weary as water in a troubled
                                               pool

    Les eny revè me my makè   lest any rob me of my mate
        Ychabbe y-yyrned sore.   for whom I have yearned so long

Betere is tholien whylė sore	to suffer badly for a time
Then mournen evermore.	
Geynest under gore,	kindest of women (lit. under a gown)
Herke to my roun.	listen to my song.
An hendy hap, etc.	

(Spelling: 'u' for 'v', 'v' for 'u', 'th' for 'þ', 'y' for 'ʒ'. Syllabized final ė dotted)

(Text adapted from G. L. Brook (ed.) (1948) *The Harley Lyrics*, Manchester University Press, rev. 1956, p. 33)

452 The third and fourth poems are by Sir Thomas Wyatt (1503?–42), the lover of Anne Boleyn before her marriage to Henry VIII.

Madam, withouten many words,
Once, I am sure, ye will or no.
And if ye will, then leave your bourds   (mockery, jests)
And use your wit and show it so.

And with a beck ye shall me call;
And if of one that burneth alway
Ye have any pity at all,
Answer him fair, with yea or nay.

If it be yea, I shall be fain;
If it be nay, friends as before;
Ye shall another man obtain,
And I mine own and yours no more.

(E. K. Chambers, *op. cit.*, p. 50.)

They flee from me that sometime did me seek
With naked foot stalking in my chamber.
I have seen them gentle, tame and meek,
That now are wild and do not remember
That sometime they put themselves in danger
    To take bread at my hand; and now they range
    Busily seeking with a continual change.

Thanked be fortune it hath been otherwise
Twenty times better; but once in special,
In thin array, after a pleasant guise,
When her loose gown from her shoulders did fall,
And she me caught in her arms long and small,
    Therewith all sweetly did me kiss
    And softly said, 'Dear heart, how like you this?'

It was no dream; I lay broad waking:
But all is turned, thorough my gentleness,
Into a strange fashion of forsaking;
And I have leave to go of her goodness,
And she also to use newfangleness
    But since that I so kindly am served,
    I would fain know what she hath deserved.

(E. K. Chambers (ed.) (1932) *The Oxford Book of Sixteenth Century Verse*, repr. 1950, p. 5.)

Discussion

453 First, a warning. There is no way of developing a real feeling for the poetry of an age except by prolonged and wide reading. Although we hope that you have enough work on Elizabethan literature later in the course to gain a taste for the poetry and drama, at the mediaeval end of things all we can hope to do is to give you a brief insight which will widen your perspective on European

cultural developments and Elizabethan poetry and drama. But if you are attracted to mediaeval poetry by anything that you read here, then I recommend the following works on poetry:

Frederick Goldin (1973) *Lyrics of the Troubadours and Trouvères*, Anchor, New York.
Brian Woledge (ed.) (1961) *The Penguin Book of French Verse*, 1.
R. T. Davies (1963) *Medieval English Lyrics*, Faber.
Brian Stone (1963) *Medieval English Verse*, Penguin Classics.

The last contains modern verse translations, but the others all give the original texts; the first two give literal modern translations, and Davies' text, which is plentifully glossed, is in modified modern spelling. All except Woledge contain substantial critical and background material. Start with the anonymous groups of songs in Woledge. Then go for the great names – Guillaume of Poitiers, Bernart de Ventadorn (the first truly *courtly* love-poet) and Arnaut Daniel among the troubadours, Benôit de Sainte-Maure, Chrétien de Troyes and especially Villon among the French; Chaucer and Skelton among the English. Most of the poems in Davies, including the best lyrics, are anonymous.

Discussion of the two mediaeval poems

454   First, the forms of the two mediaeval poems. Did you notice their extraordinary formal complexity? In Guillaume, the six-line stanza with the same three rhyme sounds running throughout the poem, thus: aabcbc, aabcbc, bbcaca, bbcaca, bbcaca. And in 'Alisoun' the same rhyme sound five times in every stanza, before a unique final sound ('baundoun', 'adoun', 'toun', 'roun') which keys and sets off the refrain, and probably the dance accompaniment as well; besides which, heavy alliteration sets up its own music and a constant expectation of more, which bursts out in the first line of the refrain. Both poets rely on a staple octosyllabic iambic line, which the English one diversifies with iambic trimeters in lines 2, 4, and 8 of the stanza, and the last line of the refrain. Such meters are especially suitable for song, but although the mediaeval poets of France, and especially Germany, often used them for narrative as well, only their extraordinary command of linguistic convention and the art of versification enabled them to maintain a narrative flow in this medium.

455   When you came to the content of these two poems, I expect you found that they differ quite sharply, except that certain standard courtly love conditions obtain in both: it is spring, and the poet is separated from his beloved and pleading with her, in the one case for a renewal of love, in the other for his passion to be returned. Guillaume is much more particular in subject-matter. Once the conventional statement about spring – foliage burgeoning, birds singing – has set the subject and tone, he is deep in the concrete actualities of his *affaire* (second stanza). There is a matter of tactics, there are memories, there is an envious watching public to take account of, the 'beautiful neighbour' is lovely and desirable by action rather than by description, and Guillaume knows how he will start making love when he next meets her in favourable circumstances. The English poet limits himself to ecstatic things, the expression of his love and beauty of Alisoun. He adopts a strict courtly love posture in accepting his suffering, and fearing the love of Alisoun for another as the worst possible thing. Did you notice the imagery on your first reading of these two poems? If not, read them again.

Discussion

456   By what we have discovered so far, we have implicitly dubbed Guillaume a competent versifier, a man of the world and an efficient lover, and the anony-

mous Englishman a passionate idealist. But the main depth and feeling in Guillaume's poem is in the beautiful image of the middle stanza, in which ordinary seasonal phenomena – the hawthorn by cold night and then by morning sunlight – typify the whole love experience. The image is linked evocatively with the return to direct fact: the word 'matí' (morning) in the first line of the fourth stanza extends the bright, early, hopeful feeling established at the end of the third stanza. And the sharp idiomatic feasting image at the end of the poem, meaning 'We can have what we want', provides an earthy finale.

457 'Alisoun' is regarded as one of the best English courtly love poems: the contrast between the pleading and lamentation of the stanzas and the pure joy of the refrain is most felicitous. But, perhaps because accidents of survival have left us very few English mediaeval secular lyrics, the impression left on me is that both Provençal and early French lyrics are much richer in content, range and imagery than English ones.

Discussion of the two Wyatt poems

458 I selected 'Madam, withouten many words' because of its haughty but common-sense treatment of courtly love, and its interesting provenance. Wyatt's poem is a fairly direct translation of a ten-line madrigal by the Italian Dragonetto Bonifacio (1500–26), and Wyatt's interest in the original, which was published in about 1535, widens the perspective within which we should view the poem to a European one. There is something much more sophisticated, in the modern sense, in the attitude of the lover than is common in mediaeval poems. The latter tend, when they are ironic, to be more, shall we say, savage. Not that the elements of 'burning' and 'pity' in this poem should be taken as other than genuine. I would have included a mediaeval example of a similar kind of thing had there been time in this short section; and when you come to your set poetry book, you will find that I draw attention to many kinds of departure, in the Elizabethan love lyric, from both the long-inherited traditions of courtly love, and the newly-dominant ones of Neo-Platonic love. (See Section 5.1 of Units 5–6, on Plato.)

459 'They flee from me that sometime did me seek' is an altogether more substantial poem, and I should like you to read it several times, and ask yourself the following questions about it:

Is it entirely, or only predominantly, or not really at all, a love poem?

How do (a) women in general (b) one woman, figure in it?

Is public life any part of the poem?

What does the poet think of himself?

What has all this to do with courtly love?

Please do not read on until you have made some sense of your responses.

Discussion

460 It would take a long paragraph to answer any one of these questions. I must suggest an approach to them all very briefly, and that will mean cutting corners and not citing evidence from the poem; which I ask you to do as you read. First, a summary, with some slight interpretation:

When the poet was in favour, lovers came to him easily, but now they have left him. He remembers one he really loved, whom he now reproaches for being like the others, following fortune in fickleness. He lost his position (in court favour as well as love?) through being gentle (i.e. noble, generous, courteous, polite), but is now ironically scornful of his former lover.

461 For me the extraordinary richness of the poem lies in its power, its mystery and its ambiguity. The poet seems caught in a web of strong, even violent, emotions in which love, lust, ambition and moral sense are inextricably entwined. It seems to me typically aristocratic to present all this within the scope of arguments of sheer power, with some nodding in the general direction of Christian (I hesitate to say courtly love) values.

462 Wyatt treats the rhyme royal stanza (check what this is from the poem) and its metre freely, submerging strict musical regularity into a kind of partly heard ground bass, and concentrating on the less regular melodies of direct and often dramatic language. This apparent looseness so upset his first editor, Tottel, that in his *Songs and Sonnets* (1557), which is known as Tottel's *Miscellany*, he made all the lines regular, often with a ridiculous effect. But Wyatt's practice in this poem is in line with that of John Donne (1573–1631) whose poetry you will sample later. After Shakespeare, these are the two Renaissance English poets who have most interested and influenced modern poets.

463 Before I leave these poems, there is a relevant social comment to make. All four depend in some measure on the mystique of knighthood. The mediaeval ones derive from the world of castle and conquest, hunt and tournament, in which the feudal writ ran. It was a world in which all the wealth of the earth, above and below, in human, animal and mineral resources, was channelled towards the nobility and the Church. The dress part of the dowry of one princess might contain miniver for which 1200 grey squirrels had had to be slaughtered, and even the lapdogs might have gold buckles on their collars (details from Joan Evans (ed.) (1966) *The Flowering of the Middle Ages*, Thames and Hudson, p. 174). The equivalent world of Wyatt is more sophisticated, more urban, and social movement seems freer; but the aristocratic hunt provides the main erotic metaphor, just as it often did in mediaeval iconography.

464 It was essential to work on texts of mediaeval courtly love poetry, because otherwise, when you come to your set poetry anthology you might take for granted an essential ingredient of Elizabethan love poetry. The typically Renaissance qualities – among them those that we associate with the spread of Neo-Platonic ideas, those that reflect early modern European court and manor life rather than mediaeval castle life, those that reflect a kind of distancing from, rather than ignorance of, religious attitudes, even those that derive self-consciously from Latin poetry – usually appear within the framework of values and attitudes of the Provençal 'invention' we have been discussing.

465 With one exception, no such detailed work is now proposed on other kinds of mediaeval poetry, and I am thinking especially of devotional, narrative and comic poetry, because these genres are of small importance in Units 29–30 (*Elizabethan Poetry*). Devotional poetry changes less during the interim than other kinds; on a short course there is no time to study full-length narrative poetry, and we have accordingly concentrated on the allegorical element in it; and as for comic poetry, if we once started on Chaucer and one or two of the anonymous fabliaux (comic tales in verse), we should probably prefer to stay in the Middle Ages. The one exception concerns preparation for part of the work of section 4 of unit 30 (Further Poems on Mutability: Death, Time and Melancholy). I should like you to read just two powerful mediaeval poems which will illuminate your contemplation of the frontispiece to Unit 30 and your study not only of poems by Raleigh, Southwell and Nashe in that section, but your future reading of almost all Elizabethan literature, including Shakespeare's plays. I offer them in their original form, one with marginal gloss and the other in modern verse translation. I hope that at some time you will further develop your acquaintance with Villon.

466   The first of these two poems is an early thirteenth-century English celebration of a typical sermon theme – exhortation to virtue fuelled by horrific description of death in sin. To judge by the number of manuscripts of it and quotations from it, it was very popular! I give my own, strictly free, verse translation, because we think it gives a better idea of the original than a prose translation.

467

Man mei longe him lives wene,
ac ofte him liyet the wreinch;
fair weder ofte him went to rene,
an ferliche maket is blench.
thar-vore, man, thu the bithench
al sel valui the grene.
wela-wey! nis king ne quene
that ne sel drinke of deth-is drench.
Man, er thu falle of thi bench,
thu sinne aquench.

Long life, O Man, you hope to gain,
Till flattened by a cunning wrench.
Your temperate weather turns to rain,
Your sun is strangely made to blench;
So here's a thought your teeth should
    clench:
'All greenness comes to withering.'
Alas! There is no queen or king
Whom draught of Death shall fail to
    drench:
Before you tumble off your bench,
    All sinning quench!

Ne mai strong ne starch ne kene
a-glye deth-is wither-clench;
yung and old and brith an-siene,
al he criveth an his streng.
vox and ferlich is the wreinch,
ne mai no man thar to-genes,
wei-la-wei! ne iweping ne bene
mede, liste, ne leches dreinch.
Man, let sinne and listes stench,
wel do, wel thench!

There's none so strong, or tough, or
    keen
That he can dodge Death's wither-
    clench:
Young and old and bright of sheen,
All, all he shatters with his strength.
Swift and fearful is his wrench:
Before it every man must quail.
Alas! No tears or prayers prevail,
No bribes, or guile, or doctor's drink;
So, Man, let sin and pleasure stink!
     Do well, so think!

Do by salomones rede,
Man, and so thu selth wel do.
Do al so he tothte and sede
what thin endinch the bring to,
ne seltu nevere mis-do.
Sore thu mith the a-drede,
wetla-wey! suich wenth wel lede
long lif and blisse under-fo.
thar deth luteth in his swo
to him for-do.

Go by Solomon the Wise,
O Man, and prosperously do;
Follow his teaching and advice,
Then you never shall misdo,
Whatever ending comes to you.
Dreading much to pay the price,
Alas! You think good deeds suffice
To bring long life and bliss to you—
But Death is lurking by your shoe
     To run you through!

Man fwi neltu the bi-thenchen?
Man fwi neltu the bisen?
of felthe thu ert isowe,
weirmes mete thu selt ben.
her navest tu blisse days thre,
al thi lif thu drist in wowe:
wela-wey deth the sal dun throwen
thar thu wenest heye ste.
In wo sal thi wele enden
in wop thi gle.

Consider, Man, how you should go,
And study in what plight you're
    thrown:
In filth you're sown, in filth you grow,
And worms shall eat you for their own.
Three days of bliss you've hardly known
On earth, and all your life is woe.
Alas! By Death you're dragged below,
Just when you thought to stay on
    throne!
You'll find your luck to misery grown,
     Your joy to moan.

Werld an wele the bi-pecheth
iwis hie buth thine ivo;
if thi werld mid wele the sliket
that is far to do the wo.
thar-fore let lust ever-gon,
man, and eft it sal the liken.

By world and wealth you're led astray;
They are your enemies, I know.
They sleek you with their gaudies gay,
To get you gripped in deathly throe.
Therefore, Man, let pleasure go,
And earn your bliss another day.

Wela-wey! hu sore him wiket
thar in one stunde other two
wurh him pine evere-mo.
 ne do man swo!

(orthotgraphy: 'v' for 'u', 'th' for 'y',
'g' or 'y' for '3')

(Adapted from Carleton Brown (ed)
(1953) *English Lyrics of the Thirteenth
Century*, Oxford.)

Alas! You yield in shameful way
Just once or twice,[1] to pleasures low,
And earn your everlasting woe.
 Man, do not so!

[1] Literally, 'in an hour or two'.

Brian Stone (1963) *Medieval English
Verse*, Penguin, pp. 64–5.

468 And the second poem, *Ballade des Dames de Temps Jadis*, by François Villon
(1431–63), is, like Wyatt's *They flee from me that sometime did me seek*, one of the
great poems of the age. No, not just of the age, but of all time. Give it a little
time please. Read it, asking yourself what elements there are in it, and how
they are fused.

469 Dites moi où, n'en quel pays
Est Flora la belle Romaine,
Archipiades, ne Thaïs,
Qui fut sa cousine germaine,
Echo, parlant quant bruit on maine
Dessus riviere ou sus estan,
Qui beauté eut trop plus
 qu'humaine.
Mais où sont les neiges d'antan?

Tell me where, or in what country, is
Flora the fair Roman girl, or Archipiades, or Thaïs, who was her counterpart, or Echo, replying whenever
sound is made over river or pool, who
had more than human beauty. But
where are last year's snows?

Où est la tres sage Heloïs
Pour qui chastré fut et puis moine
Pierre Esbaillart à Saint Denis?
Pour son amour eut ceste essoine.
Semblablement, où est la roine
Qui commanda que Buridan
Fust jeté en un sac en Seine?
Mais où sont les neiges d'antan?

Where is that wisest lady Heloise, for
whose sake Pierre Abelard was first
castrated, then became a monk at
Saint-Denis? It was through love that he
suffered this misfortune. And where,
too, is the queen who ordered Buridan
to be thrown into the Seine in a sack?
But where are last year's snows?

La roine Blanche comme lis
Qui chantoit à vois de seraine,
Berte au grant pié, Bietris, Alis,
Haremburgis qui tint le Maine.
Et Jehanne la bonne Lorraine
Qu'Anglois brulerant à Rouan;
Où sont ils, où, Vierge souvraine?
Mais où sont les neiges d'antan?

Queen Blanche, white as a lily, who
sang with a siren's voice, Berte of the
big foot, Beatrice, Alice, Haremburgis,
who ruled over Maine, and Joan the
good maid of Lorraine, who was burnt
by the English at Rouen, where are
they, where, oh! sovereign Virgin? But
where are last year's snows?

Prince, n'enquerez de semaine
Où elles sont, ne de cest an,
Qa'à ce refrain ne vous remaine:
"Mais où sont les neiges d'antan" . . .

Prince, do not ask within the week
where they are, nor within this year, or
I shall quote you this refrain: "But
where are last year's snows?" . . .

Puis que papes, rois, fils de rois
Et conceus en ventres de roines,
Sont ensevelis morts et frois,
(En autrui mains passent leurs
 regnes)
Moi, povre mercerot de Rennes,
Mourrai je pas? Oui, se Dieu plaist;
Mais que j'aie fait mes estrennes,
Honneste mort ne me desplaist.

Since popes, kings, and sons of kings
conceived in the womb of queens are
buried, dead and cold, and their
kingdoms pass into the hands of others,
I, a poor pedlar of Rennes, shall I not
die? Yes, if it please God; provided
that I have had my fling, an honourable
death is not displeasing to me.

Ce monde n'est perpetuel,
Quoi que pense riche pillart:
Tous sommes sous mortel coutel.
Ce confort prent povre vieillart,
Lequel d'estre plaisant raillart
Eut le bruit, lors que jeune estoit,
Qu'on tendroit à fol et paillart,
Se, vieil, à railler se mettoit.

Or lui convient il mendier,
Car à ce force le contraint.
Regrete hui sa mort et hier,
Tristesse son cuer si estraint;
Se, souvent, n'estoit Dieu qu'il
   craint,
Il feroit un horrible fait;
Et advient qu'en ce Dieu enfraint
Et que lui mesme se desfait.

Car s'en jeunesse il fut plaisant,
Ore plus rien ne dit qui plaise:
(Toujours vieil singe est desplaisant,
Moue ne fait qui ne desplaise).
S'il se tait, afin qu'il complaise,
Il est tenu pour fol recreu;
S'il parle, on lui dit qu'il se taise
Et qu'en son prunier n'a pas creu.

Aussi ces povres femmelettes
Qui vieilles sont et n'ont de quoi,
Quant ils voient ces pucelettes
Emprunter elles, à requoi
Ils demandent à Dieu pourquoi
Si tost naquirent, n'à quel droit.
Nostre Seigneur se taist tout quoi,
Car au tancer il le perdroit.

This world is not eternal, whatever the rich extortioner may think. Above us all is the fatal knife. That thought comforts the poor old man, who was renowned as a gay jester in his youth, and who would be considered both a fool and a libertine if he took to joking in his old age.

Now he must beg, for he is brought to it by necessity; he longs for death today and yesterday, sorrow so weighs upon his heart. Often, were it not for his fear of God, he would do a horrible deed, and it may happen that in this matter he trespasses against God and does away with himself.

For if he was amusing in his youth, now he can never say anything that pleases (an old monkey is always ugly, he cannot make any but an ugly face). If he hopes to win favour by keeping silent, he is considered a poor, weak fool; if he speaks, he is told to be quiet and not to behave like an idiot.

And these poor little women who are old and have nothing to live on, when they see the young girls supplanting them, within their hearts they ask God why they were born so soon, and by what right. Our Lord is silent and gives no reply, for if it came to a dispute He would lose.

(*Penguin Book of French Verse*, Vol. 1.)

Discussion

mutable:– subject to change. inconstant

470 The whole poem is on the theme of mutability ('The lamentable change is from the best' says Edgar, in *King Lear* at the beginning of Act IV), a favourite subject throughout the period, and one which produces many of the Elizabethan poems you will study. But this poem starts with a catalogue of famous beauties and events drawn from classical and early mediaeval times, and their attributes come from the world of courtly love: Heloise's suffering in love, Blanche's siren voice. A prevailing religious tone threads the poem, with an invocation to the virgin, and constant references to God. The secular prince, most glamorous object of death's attention, is also invoked in the four-line separate stanza. Against this background, a conventional one sharp with detail and eloquent in its refrain about last year's snows, the poet presses his own predicament of decay and poverty. At the end, when all declining humanity after a glorious but suffering past, is lined up in its indignity for the final stroke, the jongleur's radical wit and judgement comes out in the defiant

Nostre Seigneur sa taist tout quoi,
Car au tancer il le perdroit.

It is a noble blasphemy prepared for by Villon's insistence earlier on such savage detail as Abelard's predicament and such comic incongruity as Berte's nickname – 'of the big foot'. You won't find all your Elizabethans as hard locked on reality as Villon.

Notes

Notes

RENAISSANCE AND REFORMATION

Historical Introduction

1
2 } The Period and its Significance

Economic and Social Developments

3
4 } Economy and Society in Western Europe 1300–1600.
The Transition from Feudalism to Capitalism

5
6 } The Mediaeval Inheritance and the Revival of Classical Learning

Florence

7   Florentine Society 1382–1494

8
9
10 } Sculpture 1400–70
Architecture: Brunelleschi and Alberti 1400–72
Painting 1300–1520

11
12
13 } Iconography
Artistic Status
Leonardo

14 Machiavelli: *The Prince* and its Historical Context

Copernicus

15
16 } The Background to Copernicus
The Copernican Revolution

Renaissance Music

17
18
19 } Renaissance Music Part 1
Renaissance Music Part 2
Renaissance Music Part 3

The Reformation

20
21 } Origins of the Reformation

22
23 } Luther and Lutheranism

24
25 } Calvin and other Reformers

26
27 } The Catholic Reformation

English Renaissance Literature

28 An Introduction to Elizabethan England

29
30 } Elizabethan Poetry

31
32 } English Renaissance Drama
Doctor Faustus, The Changeling, The Alchemist

33
34 } *King Lear*